"Stephen Levine offers a beautiful collection of stories for the heart, weaving his personal experiences with animals and the teachings gleaned from those experiences. Animals, through their natural instinctive behavior and closer connection to the natural world, serve to remind us that we too are creatures of nature—and, in spite of our intellect and self-reflective consciousness, we too are instinctual beings. You will thoroughly enjoy these tales and carry their lessons with you in a way that opens your heart and mind to the teachings from the animals." —STEVEN FARMER, AUTHOR OF *Animal Spirit Guides* and *Messages from Your Animal Spirit Guides* oracle cards

"This small treasure of a book is about the better animals of our nature. Whether it is forgiveness from a salamander, stillness from a green snake, the acknowledgement of territories by a spider or mindfulness by ravens, over and over these stories lead us, too, to realize the primacy of kindness as the way for all of us to help each other to arrive at wellbeing. Ajahn Chah used to say, 'Everything is teaching us, if we let it.' This slender volume carries that exact same message. The lesson might be sweet, like the results of practicing patience in caring for a sick cat, or it might be bitter, like the witnessing of a weeping bull before an impassioned crowd—either way, how much better our world will be if we allow the animals of our own nature to learn from the life that is all around us." —AJAHN AMARO, AMARAVATI BUDDHIST MONASTERY

"A beautifully wise and whimsical book that brings us back into our hearts and connects us with the everything. Many authors talk about mindfulness, but we are left unaffected. Stephen has a magical way of bringing us into the experience itself. Even from the beyond, he calls

us home to ourselves. As I read his poignant stories, I was reminded of what really mattered. I am grateful for this brilliant offering."
—JEFF BROWN, AUTHOR OF *Soulshaping and Grounded Spirituality*

"Stephen's generosity of spirit and depth of compassion shine forth. Read these stories and you will see this world and your place in it in a new, fresh way. What a sweet gift!" —DALE BORGLUM, LIVING/DYING PROJECT

"French poet and novelist Anatole France wrote: 'Until one has loved an animal, a part of one's soul remains unawakened.' Spiritual teacher Eckart Tolle says, 'I have lived with several Zen masters—all of them cats.' French writer Milan Kundra says, 'Dogs are our link to Paradise. They don't know evil or jealousy or discontent.' Jewish philosopher Martin Buber wrote: 'An animal's eyes have the power to speak a great language.' These words all ring true to me, as the animals in my own life have been wise teachers, loyal companions, and loving friends. I know what Stephen Levine means when he talks about his 'life becoming truer due to the interchange with plants and animals, mercy and awareness.' Mine, too. I'm happy and grateful that Stephen wrote this wonderful book. I love it!" —BJ GALLAGHER, COAUTHOR OF *A Peacock in the Land of Penguins: A Fable About Creativity and Courage*

"Stephen Levine's *Animal Sutras* resonates at the deepest level of heart and soul, invoking memories of our own joyful and painful experiences with the four-legged, winged, finned, and slithering. His vivid prose delights, as he reveals profound insights on the relationship between all sentient beings. This meaningful collection will move you from teary-eyed to grinning like a Cheshire cat as he lovingly describes his wonder-filled menagerie." —SARAH BOWEN, AUTHOR OF *Spiritual Rebel: A Positively Addictive Guide to Finding Deeper Perspective and Higher Purpose*

ANIMAL SUTRAS

ANIMAL SUTRAS

ANIMAL SPIRIT STORIES

Stephen Levine

Foreword by JOANNE CACCIATORE, PH.D.
Illustrations by SUSAN PIPERATO

MONKFISH BOOK PUBLISHING COMPANY
RHINEBECK, NY

Animal Sutras: Animal Spirit Stories © 2019 by Stephen Levine

Hardcover ISBN 978-1-948626-06-4
ebook ISBN 978-1-948626-07-1

Library of Congress Cataloging-in-Publication Data

Names: Levine, Stephen, 1937-2016 author.
Title: Animal sutras : animal spirit stories / Stephen Levine ; foreword by
    Joanne Cacciatore, Ph.D. ; illustrations by Susan Piperato.
Description: Rhinebeck, New York : Monkfish Book Publishing Company, 2019.
Identifiers: LCCN 2019011202 (print) | ISBN 9781948626064 (hardcover : alk.
    paper)
Subjects: LCSH: Animals--Religious aspects. | Human-animal
    relationships--Religious aspects. | Nature--Religious aspects.
Classification: LCC BL439 .L48 2019 (print) | LCC BL439 (ebook) | DDC
    202/.12--dc23
LC record available at https://lccn.loc.gov/2019011202
LC ebook record available at https://lccn.loc.gov/2019980040

Illustrations by Susan Piperato
Book design by Colin Rolfe

Monkfish Book Publishing Company
22 East Market Street, Suite 304
Rhinebeck, NY 12572
(845) 876-4861
monkfishpublishing.com

CONTENTS

TABLE OF CONTENTS

"Things are quiet here. Spring begins to overflow into the valley and crawls up the side of the mountain. The buzzards and the hummingbirds have noticed, returning about an hour apart. The seasonal stream is trickling. Coyotes run the ridge with new cubs. And something greater than us all calls to us to make peace in the torn world, to learn to love even when we are in pain, even when we are frightened, to consider the wellbeing of others as we might that of our own children, and the prayer becomes May All Beings Be Free From Suffering, May All Beings Be At Peace."

—Stephen Levine

FOREWORD

BRINGING MERCY TO A BROKEN WORLD

To truly love, and to be loved, is the heart's greatest desire; to show and to receive compassion, especially when in the midst of feeling deep grief and pain, is one of our most exigent needs. Yet this hallowed space of love and compassion is sometimes overlaid with the complexities of modernity; demands on our time; a lack of attention and awareness; past wounds that quietly follow the unawakened heart; and, ultimately, a sense of disconnection from self, other, and the space between. This space between self and other, and the sutra that unifies all beings, is hallowed space.

There is perhaps no more elegiac narrative of this sacred Oneness than Stephen Levine's *Animal Sutras*. Stephen—at a cellular level—understood that what we do to the other, even the animal other, we also do to ourselves and to our kin. This beautiful yet painful truth is hidden beneath the disconnected hedonism and materialism of our world. To speak this truth is both brave and necessary for our species, for all beings, and for our planet.

And so, in this posthumously published book, with tenderness and verity, Stephen invites readers into the mystical space of connection with all that is, all that has ever been, and all that will ever be on this Earth that we call home. *Animal Sutras* is an open-hearted and vulnerable, even apologetic and at times humorous, exploration of our essential connection to our four-legged, winged, and crawling brethren. Few mystics and even fewer scholars have sought to understand the mystical import of animals in the cultivation of meaning and purpose in our lives. The intimate relationship between animals, the natural world, and humans underlies the very matrix of our existence, yet too many humans remain asleep, unaware of what Stephen called its "elemental presence." This presence contains the consciousness of Oneness, the "open secret" that calls to us, and there is a grace and mercy inherent in answering that call. Stephen, over and over again throughout his life, willingly turned toward and answered that call.

Engaging nature as metaphor, both literal and figurative, Stephen's writing helps us feel. Not better. Not different. Just *feel*. The shift in the reader arises from feeling to seeing—and perceiving—beyond the superficial. When we feel our pain, our grief, our losses and when we can fully inhabit them, that inhabitation—that being with what is—can then be transformed into the numinous nexus about which he teaches. We suffer, like all sentient beings, and that suffering which connects us, when lived fully, can shatter our hearts open to the suffering of all. What use of pain could be more meaningful, more worthy of the very wound that caused the pain? Shards of our shattered hearts can land softly around us, bringing "mercy and awareness" to a much-broken world. The invitation first, though, is to stay with it, to remain bravely with the horror and beauty of our existence, and to turn toward the reality of our finitude. From that, from the center of our very humanity, is the truth of that Oneness which Stephen describes.

He recounts this mercy and awareness in story after story of mysteriously profound animal encounters, historic and contemporaneous, feeling self-forgiveness through shared moments with a salamander, humble learning through the great teachings of the raven, and miraculous surprises through a half-paralyzed cat named Shoebox who gave birth in his ear at 3:00 a.m. There is an organic joy—and also, at times, a sadness—in Stephen's stories that gives rise to a sense of awe in the reader. With rich descriptions of both his ordinary and extraordinary days, he invites us to contemplate deeply the simple yet complex wonder of life and being and liberation, including a momentary encounter with a skunk he'd wanted to kill to protect his chicks. Instead, under the influence of the Perseid meteor shower, face to face with the murderous critter, he demonstrated mercy and merely fortified the chicks' enclosure while the skunk "kept on singing." If we pause, if we allow time and space to slowly unfold between self and other, we will be changed by our encounter with animals, as Stephen was so many times.

"Humans are a savage lot, though capable of grace."

I, myself, have had many indescribable direct experiences with animals. I stopped eating animals in 1972, when I was only seven years old, and went vegan years later. Throughout my life, wild birds, wounded bunnies, homeless dogs, and other creatures, perhaps sensing my respect for the worthiness of their fragile lives, have been drawn to share space with me. This is something for which I am deeply grateful and by which I am humbled. But perhaps no more direct experience affected me the same way as my encounter with a pack-horse in April 2015. He was emaciated, dehydrated, with exposed spinal bones protruding from his skin and open wounds revealing underlying the muscles on both sides of his girth. Strike-marks scarred his body, some of them freshly oozing blood and pus. He had been carrying at least 100 pounds of weight up a treacherous trail when he collapsed, and he was very close to death.

As with Stephen's encounter with the dying deer he met while riding his horse, Duster, I felt, viscerally, the original sensate of Oneness like never before when I looked into this horse's nearly dead, wholly vacant, eyes. I was this horse, and this horse was me. His suffering was mine, and mine was his.

This chance encounter with a tortured horse happened two decades after the death of my child in 1994. I, too, was tortured. As I sat with the wounded horse on the trail, I remembered experiencing acute hopelessness, despair, trauma, and fear— exactly what I knew this horse was feeling—in the marrow of my bones. It was a primal pain that eludes words, a wound that I have kept intentionally open all these years so that I can feel, deeply, the pain of others. No doubt, the presence of intense pain, whether it is physical or emotional, as Stephen experienced in his spattering of poison oak, shifts our "fascinated seeing" and perception of everything.

"Resting in the dappled shadow of an ample tree, we sit quietly, reflecting on how hardened our belly has become, fruitlessly trying to protect itself from pain. And honoring the pain-ridden abdominal muscles holding the grief long-stored in our belly, we send the bear of mercy to bring loving kindness into it.

"It takes a while to get out of our own way and become quiet as a bear silently surveying its surroundings. Slowly, what was invisible

becomes visible. An ant purposefully scouting for the tribe. A bee testing pollen. A cloud that reminds us of something. Gradually, what was unheard attracts the inner ear. Bird songs vary. The wind sings differently from tree to tree. We settle through levels and levels of quiet. We breathe in warmth and mercy, slowly, patiently, through those great bear nostrils, breathing out the holding, the forgetfulness, the mercilessness, which shadows us."

It is one thing to believe in Oneness: and it is an entirely other matter to *experience* Oneness. Leaving the abused, nearly dead horse on the trail that day, abandoned and alone and helpless, was like leaving myself. I wept for us both, as victim and as witness, realizing that I could not avert my gaze and unsee what I had seen. The horse was there, in that particular moment in time, and our paths were crossing. My duty to him, and to myself, I knew, was to fight for his life. And so, I fought to save him. With every shred of energy that I could muster, I fought for his life. As if he was my child, as if he was me, I fought for him. Through tears and sleepless nights, unanswered phone calls and emails, I persisted. Three days later, I was able to rescue this horse, who now lives in his own sanctuary with seventeen other rescue animals. The Selah House Respite Center and Carefarm, on ten irrigated acres in Cornville, Arizona, is a place where formerly tortured and abused animals can come to know only love and compassion. I named the pack-horse Chemakoh and, as fate or perhaps Oneness would have it, he now helps the broken hearts of grieving parents who come to the farm from around the world, by "offer(ing) his energies in response to love" and even grief. As Stephen has taught us, both in word and in deed, this is just as it should be.

"...the deeper we go the less definable we become."

This book is like holding hallowed space between your fingers; with each turn of the page comes a new breath of mercy and awareness. Stephen's teachings are an answer to the fast-paced trivialities of modern life, a retort to shallow spiritual practice, and a rejoinder to the consumeristic demands on our time. He begs our attention to the moment, calls our attention toward the future, and compels us to see, with clarity, our ancient wounds which, if tended, can open us to Oneness like no other conjured or created experience in our lives. Only then can we use our pain as a conduit to the pain and fear and grief of another, whether that other is human, animal, or the Earth. And only then will we have gained the wisdom of the sutra that unifies all beings.

Animal Sutras is a magnum opus of love and Oneness, of mercy and awareness. May we all embody these teachings with fierce, and fearless, compassion. May all beings be at peace.

—*Joanne Cacciatore, Ph.D.*

INTRODUCTION

THIRTY-FIVE YEARS AGO, I was so moved by the Jataka tales—hundreds of anecdotes and fables which depict earlier incarnations of the future Buddha, Siddhartha Gautama—that I considered setting up a publishing company to bring to a wider public a new version/translation of these wonderful, inspiring stories. Included were stories of animals teaching people, and people using animals to make a point—stories of earlier incarnations of the Buddha practicing compassion in the animal and human realm.

Instead, over the next few years, we began the Mindfulness Series for Unity Press. We published books reprinted from the Theravada publishing group in India as well as books by Jack Kornfield, Sujata, and Joseph Goldstein for some years, until I was invited to teach Buddhist meditation practice by some of those mentioned.

Animals have a natural mindfulness: They know what they are doing. Humans, who are full of confusion and seldom wholly in touch with their mind/body, need encouragement and technique to live in the present. As Rumi said, "Love is the bridge."

Now, in my seventieth year, I have begun collecting a few of my animal spirit stories published over the last forty years, from the green snake of my youth that first taught me the meditative stillness, to the spiders that taught trust and patience, to my return after a great loss to my cabin in the woods, where I found my heart patiently waiting. I include these stories along with a number of precious teachings and transcendent moments that I shared with animals while I worked for the Nature Conservancy in the '70s, while I was tending a wildlife sanctuary in southern Arizona. Also coming onto these pages are the past twenty years of our living on the land surrounded by the Carson National Forest and the Picuris Pueblo in northern New Mexico, sharing the side of the mountain with elk and foxes and the lion that cries like a widow; and the dusty horned toad, its blood warming serene by the morning path; the coyote and jack rabbit, born to trace each other in the snow; the teaching raven and the moonlit skunk; the mouse of faith and the bear of compassion.

The primary teaching of the Jataka tales is generosity. The collection of stories calls to us to overcome the human tendency to separate and attempt to control. It teaches the sweetness of renunciation: the giving of oneself to another, for the benefit of all. It is the lineage of the unfolding of generosity, kindness, and insight through the auspices of the evolution of consciousness, just as in the story of an ancient king who, having had an epiphany and a blossoming of care for those who were most in need, gave away all his wealth to the poor. But then, standing and surveying the effects of his largess, he noticed the hunger of the mosquitoes buzzing about him and offered them his body and blood to feed on.

The Jataka tales are stories of commitment and self-sacrifice in the time when the cosmic egg cracks, and being loving becomes even more important than being loved. There is no martyrdom in these stories, just a sense of finishing one labor after another in the clearing of the field of awareness, on the path toward the healing we took birth for, as when the Buddha-in-training throws himself in a leap of compassion in front of a starving tigress, saving her life and providing milk for her cubs.

A *sutra* is a thread or rope that holds things together as in the connection between humankind and nature, between the conditioned mind and the boundless spirit. These animal sutras differ from the Jataka tales. While the Jakata tales are myths and fables, these stories are the living truths transmitted from the presence of nature in my life, the stories of a life—my own—becoming truer due to my interchanges with plants and animals, and my resulting experiences of mercy and awareness.

At the wisdom door we are told to pay particular attention to the process of placing oneself in the position of others in order to promote selflessness and compassion. "Whoever wishes for salvation should practice the supreme mystery—the exchanging of himself and the other."

It is in approaching this sharing of consciousness that the joy of plants and animals, water and stone, arises—in the unity that we call, for lack of a better term, *love*. It is from that meeting in the outer orbits of loving kindness and concern for the wellbeing of others that we receive these teachings at the center, and these stories here are told.

—*Stephen Levine*
Chamisal, New Mexico, 2007

Part 1

YOUTH

1. EVOLUTION

WE ALL ORIGINATE FROM ONE GE-
NUS: consciousness.
In the course of evolution, as reptiles
evolved into birds, they began to dream.
What a leap into the expanse of the inner world!
And in that revolutionary/evolutionary leap of awareness, the
mind sees through the shadows that pass for reality and discovers a bit more about fire and what Krishnamurti called "the
flame of awareness."

This jump from reptile to bird is so enormous in the ex-
pansion of consciousness and the spirit that it manifests, as in
Jung's collective unconscious, within the poetry and religion
of many separate cultures. The reptile/bird expresses the energetic metamorphosis of animal to human and from human
to God and God to pure light in such disparate societies as
the North American tribal peoples, Hindu, Chinese, Buddhist,
Bonn, and many others.

Evolution creates a forward participation in the senses.
Black Elk speaks of humanity no longer living in the "shadows
cast by reality." Turning, we see the light of day, the glow of
night. Imagine expanding our world the way that chasm-cross-
ing longing of the maturation of the body/mind expanded to
contain the flying spirit. And it wasn't just dreaming that accompanied that leap from reptile to bird; obviously, the flying

spirit also created wings. It went from the long belly, cold against the cold ground, to a warming in the blood and a lifting up—flight came to the lizard. This forward motion was so great, so momentous, so immensely promising, that the sprouting of wings by the slow-witted earthbound leading edge of evolution was depicted as the fire-breathing (warm-blooded), long-scaled, writhing, powerfully-winged dragon. In Asian cultures, the dragon is often used to represent wisdom, transcendence, and eternity—or even deeper, timelessness—and the manifest mystery of greater and greater participation in the senses. In Central America, Quetzalcoatl, the Aztec's plumed serpent, is the guardian of this momentous transformation from the earth element to the air element. And the transformation of land beast to water-held whale is completed, the forelegs grown to flippers: what must that inner transformation of consciousness be like when the earth element enters into the becoming of water?

And what great changes lie ahead in our capacities? Imagine such an expanse in our world. The next leap could perhaps incorporate, rather than attempting to exceed our previous learnings and abilities. Humans would retrieve the sense of beauty. The warm breeze would be filled with the fragrances and odors of the world; our seeing and hearing, smelling and tasting, thinking and dreaming would all swim together. We would no longer be censoring the scintillation of energy vibrating in the alpine meadow, but instead would feel in the whole of our inner world the changing shapes in clouds, and experience a considerable sense of safety while lying beside a trusted friend or perhaps a mate. Simple kindness would evolve to profound mercy, with the inner world melting at the edge as the Eye of Beauty opened, and the fear that constricted around it and limited its focal length softened into trust in the process.

And when did flight and dream combine in that first rhythmic line, that first chant singing of birth and death, love and loss? When did the first poem warm the blood of language? And when, in perhaps the greatest of forward leaps, did we become aware we were *aware*? When, as the Sufis might put it, did we approach the "open secret"? When did we realize consciousness and, further yet, note its constituent awareness? It may well be that what are called "spiritual practices" are the dynamism of the flying spirit propelling itself forward, that meditation and focused contemplation, chant and yogic edge-playing are stimuli at the forward edge, opening the new warm-bloodedness of compassion, the flights of imaginings presently beyond our imagination, the censor barriers withdrawn to allow us to see more of the worlds we inhabit.

The unfolding continually attempts to reach beyond itself toward what is to be seen and heard, felt, and known expands.

2. PREQUEL

I HAVE, FOR MOST OF MY LIFE, received remarkable teachings in how to be a human being from the animal spirits.

It was their invitation that began my opening, and it is still the quality of wholeness that I experienced with the animal spirits on the land that regulates the beat of my heart.

When I first heard someone say that in fifty years all the songbirds might be extinct, I worried about that song that I had learned so long ago from the thrushes as I was waking up as a child, listening silent in my warm morning bed.

It breaks my heart to recall that robin that I shot with my BB gun, my pride of accuracy instantly vanishing when I saw the torn bird lying empty of life on the grass.

If there are no birds, who will transmit from the ledge outside the frightened child's window that, somehow, everything is going to be okay, that we are an integral part of something very big and indescribably beautiful?

* * *

Nature is our first awakening to an elemental presence all about us, absent nowhere. Even in a dying tree or the skeleton of the king snake in a knothole crevice, there is energy moving one thought into the next, precisely the same as it moves the clouds across the sky: a living movement and grace in its wake. Birdsong is often most easily heard and certainly most quickly recognized in nature. I feel overwhelming appreciation, even for the scattered feathers of that tiny sweat owl we were talking with a few days before.

Ramakrishna said his first ecstasy as a child happened when he "became lost seeing one morning a vast sunrise and a flock of passing birds." Indeed, there are initiations in the forest that teach us how to sit quietly and simply *be*; and from songs learned from the wind-shaken sage on the mesa, or the brittle grass rattle by the dry stream bed. From the first rippling of summer's initiatory monsoon, we take the teaching in the watery essence of things alive and less. On the trail, half a cottontail draped over a low branch of a young *piñon*, left for tomorrow's supper by the gray fox denning beneath a great outcropping, reminds me to take along lunch for myself on my next walk. Nature can teach us what we are afraid of and how to work with it. It teaches us how to be true to ourselves.

And nature holds teachings in birth and death. "Letting go is a teaching in trust and patience," a woman told me as I cared for her as she was dying, repeating what Jesus, standing there in the shadows, had just said to her.

* * *

Sometimes the restorative power of nature has to reach out for us, to remind us of the enormity of our Being. In the cities, pigeons coo on the ledge outside our window, but we do not hear them; stone walls block the inner recesses of perception. But even on the tenth floor of a building in the midst of New York City forty years ago, their calling reminded me of my deeper nature.

When I lay down to nap a bit, lost in the concrete canyons of my youthful miscreancy, I did not at first recognize salvation playing at my ears. Deterred from sleep by an upwelling in the mind, I had no sense that when I stood up again, I would be a poet.

Lying on the couch, listening to the coo of the pigeons patrolling the ledge outside my window, I found my breath. Within the breath was a passageway to the heart, which the pigeons seemed to be calling me toward, a path through the morass of self-conscious I had long been seeking. My breath kept time to the murmuring just outside my window. My breath and the Earth's breath were in perfect harmony, reconnecting me with the planet and the animal spirits therein, which were my first deep muses. Lying there on the couch, my first poems began spontaneously to recite themselves from the unfolding of the heart.

Each day thereafter, a poem arose in praise of the enormity into which I found I fit so perfectly.

Until then, I had not recognized that I had gradually lost that primal connection with the natural world I had experienced so strongly in my youth.

Taking a walk in Central Park, I felt myself being drawn by the taste of chlorophyll and the shriek of a blade of grass pressed against the lips—I was reconnecting with the Earth, even on the very Upper West Side of Manhattan.

Such experiences of *interbeing*—that sense of deep, even profound, interconnectedness, which often causes an overwhelming feeling of Oneness to arise—increase confidence in the possibility of a true and deep healing.

This draw toward our common natural center, and the poetry which praises it, offered considerable insight for me into the healing of the mind and the opening of the heart as something one must do for themselves no matter the guidance. "The work to be done, the grace we are!" murmured the pigeon chorus.

3. SNAKES

 I HAVE A LONG HISTORY WITH SNAKES. As a child, I swam in Lake Winnipesaukee, in New Hampshire, diving for large, smooth, broad-headed water snakes that were fat with fish and frogs, which, much of the time, my camp buddy Terry and I caught by latching them onto our outstretched arms and dragging them into the rowboat. Terry caught "Grandpa Snakee," which he took home to Brooklyn with him (his mother, I suspect, was as pleased as mine was when I showed her my summer catch), and found out at the Bronx Zoo that it was just two inches short of a record.

That summer, as I entered puberty, the test of manhood was plowing toward me with its head extended above the waters of our trembling selfhood.

We left no log unturned, no fallen board or branch unmoved in our quest for the smooth, cool touch of the grass and water snakes, and the bull, milk, garter, king, big black racer, and corn snakes.

Indeed, in my thirteen-year-old mind, being the outsider I always felt myself to be, I became quite attached to a small, emerald-green grass snake, "Greenie," that I felt I communicated with, feeding him ant eggs and inviting him to reside in my shirt pocket for a couple of weeks. He even remained in my shirt pocket when I slept—my first yoga was learning to be still in my sleep on my back, not to turn and perhaps roll over on Greenie. After I completed whatever initiation was to be had from so small a creature in so big a world about the perfect beauty in nature, he took off one night. I was much the wiser for our relationship. He had taught me to be still.

I thought, as I slalomed through adolescence, that I would become a herpetologist and make the study of reptiles my life's work. I was encouraged in these endeavors by my parents, who also were relieved, I suspect, hoping that it might draw me away from my interests in chemistry and my lab in the cellar in which there had already been two explosions—I'd been provided with chemicals, flasks, and burners by my chemist father. I think they wanted most, even more than to encourage my study of snakes, was to leave their home unexploded. As a teenager, my interest in science, which was noticed by my teachers, allowed me to take college classes in the New York State teachers college associated with the high school I attended. I went to lectures and met the great herpetologist Raymond Ditmars, and I wrote to Dr. T. Van, the director of the Bronx Zoo, and was invited to visit.

The other day, while walking by the stream, my attention was drawn to the diaphanous skin shed by a bull snake. Sitting by the slightly singing stream under the green canopy of summer, my mind filled that empty skin, my attention fitting perfectly within. Fossils are imprints set in stone, composed out of the earth element—a teaching in the long trail of time that has brought us to this living moment. Some creatures, however, leave but an airy mark in time, a glistening bit of well-designed protoplasm trembled by the breeze: they are a teaching in impermanence. The snake's shed skin says that sometimes even time is left behind—only the present moment is real and all the rest is a dream about the egg from which we hatched and the many skins we will shed on our way to completion.

The shed skin speaks of how our sole identification with the superficial—the outer body, composed of a few thin cells—delays our entrance into the real body that lies beneath, the life body that holds our acquired exterior in place.

My anticipated university training had great support and good recommendations. But then the powerful Kundalini energy depicted in Asia as a serpent, regarded as the seat of the life force, said to be coiled at the base of the spine, began to rise within me past the realms of survival and sex and my acquired personage in the world. Over the next years, it began softening in me and releasing the fearful armoring that we carry in the belly, which uncoils from the belly to the heart, occasionally passing through hell on the way to heaven, through our collective isolation to the awaiting communion, to a new life accompanied by the opening of the Eye of Beauty and the start of singing. The origin of my song was revealed. My song had perhaps begun decades before with that little, emerald-green grass snake.

The only frame of reference I had for this spiritual upwelling, this awakening, was from the green snake's sleep teachings, and my learning to surrender the restlessness of adolescence so as not to injure another. Somehow, not holding onto pride or resistance (therefore experiencing grace), like a snake shedding his skin as he grew, I allowed the bright new energy to pass on through without getting stuck in some neuron-cluster or loose filament in the body dug by the fear of the mind, and without causing difficulties in finding another nesting place, or perhaps even experiencing illness. Spiritual pride is like a pit viper in flowered grass.

The snake sheds its skin because there is not room enough within the skin for it to grow. This is a clear-eyed teaching on the benefits of change, and how, on another level, as the heart expands, it finds itself in a greater body, acting for the benefit of a larger world. The snake is only able to receive nourishment from what it has ingested if it finds a source of warmth, most often accompanied by a source of light. This is an object lesson that, with little or no distortion, exemplifies that in a life without warmth and light (mercy and wisdom), we decompose. When these charms, mercy and wisdom, are present—whether through our caring for a fragile wildling or our holding the hand of a young mother dying of cancer—we feel the pulse of the universe in our fingertips. A star-nosed mole momentarily understands everything and becomes preternaturally patient, becomes the pulse of evolution. The ticking of change.

* * *

Before I can leave this story, I must make an act of contrition:

I must ask the forgiveness of two snakes I killed: one forty years ago, one a few years ago.

The first was a six-foot black racer on the cliff above Monterey Bay beside Steinbeck's Watsonville.

Great Granddad Snake, winding out of the flowering ice plant, you were sacrificed to make a talisman, a medicine bag for a friend. I dried your shimmering skin in the sun. I ask your forgiveness.

The second was a rattlesnake hunkered down in the rocks beside the house where our grandchildren sometimes play. We asked it to leave all day long, pulling the dogs away from it repeatedly. We sent *metta,* loving kindness, to it on and off during the night and hoped for its safe retreat. But in the morning it was still there, just out of reach.

I did not know what else to do, with the children's visiting weekend approaching. The noise startled the dogs. I ask your forgiveness.

* * *

JULY 11

This morning I kill the Beloved in the backyard with a
shotgun.
He comes as a timber rattlesnake this time
to test the heart, to see what remains in the karmic bundle.
He wishes me no harm, only death.
I lean down to look into his eyes,
to try to make contact, a slit of onyx
in a glistening amber field,
but he does not like that, and coils to strike,
a sacred articulation in each rising vertebra,
the hiss and rattle of the Nagas,
or of the demons in Milarepa's cave,
trying to draw the saint's attention away
from the healing buried in his body.
The serpent three times throws himself forward and draws
himself back.
In his open mouth is the seed syllable "hum."
He is the living Uroborus, mending our broken world
by intentionally completing the sacred hoop.
He wishes only to evolve, to dream.
He is a moment of energy teetering on the edge of eternity.
    Serpent, back to the heavens with you!
    Serpent, tell them we won't be long....

* * *

Some years ago, Coyote Trickster, as our Pueblo neighbors
might say, played a serpentine trick on us. Ondrea was driving,

and out of the heating vent near the floor on my side of the front seat I saw the head of a snake appear. I thought at first she might be playing a practical joke on me with a rubber snake, but the snake kept drawing itself out through the vent onto the floor of the car. I asked Ondrea to stop, to pull over, to get out of the car! But she thought I was just kidding about a snake in the car—a practical joke from me—and kept driving.

With some urgency, I suggested we'd better get out of the car. But Ondrea was not clearly seeing the markings of one of our local rattlesnakes, which had probably followed the scent of a mouse up into the engine compartment when the car was parked. I had to reach over and tap her on the elbow to please look over before we were going to be forced out of the car in some Keystone-cops tumble on the side of the road. By now, about four feet of the six-footer had made its way into the cab. Ondrea looked over, the car wobbled a bit, and we pulled quickly to the side and jumped out of the now snake-inhabited SUV. It was a gopher snake, fake rattles and all. We invited the harmless creature (something of a poser) out of the car next to a grassy meadow.

We still laugh about that one. I learned a lesson and received another moment of serpent wisdom.

* * *

And then there was the lovely congregation of garter snakes in an old cemetery behind an old white clapboard church down the road from Ondrea's parents in New Hampshire. Ondrea and I have long had an aesthetic and heart-nourishing interest in old cemeteries, ever since we saw a small family plot from the eighteenth century whose tombstone read:

Remember friends, as you pass by
As you are now, so once so was I.
As I am now, so you must be.
Prepare yourself to follow me.

Practicing mindfulness and mercy is the perfect preparation for death. And so, for some reason, perhaps the recent rains or some underground disturbance, multiple shiny, excessively harmless garter snakes appeared that day in the old New Hampshire cemetery, coming from around and under numerous gravestones. We had never seen anything like it. There may have been a hundred swaying, tumbling, racing, lovemaking Olympic participants. And they were friendlier than the human base-reptilian brain often allows. So we sat down on the grass and let a number of them ordain us with that particular, almost magical "included" feeling of a snake gliding through our fingers and hands.

After we received the blessing of the extraordinary parishioners behind the church, exorcising Eden's curse, and we sang a few hymns to the inexpressible joy of nature, we returned to Ondrea's parents' house for soup.

* * *

Surrounding the planet is the Uroborus, the alchemical serpent with its tail in its mouth—the dragon of the interstice, the leaper of species, containing the secrets of turning dross to gold, of the enlightenment of minerals and all sentient beings. The snake is evolution, and we are the snake before dreaming gave us the rest of us.

4. T H E   L O O N S

WHERE DO THE LOONS GO in winter? Their resting ground is as yet undiscovered; they migrate into the unknown. Passing overhead, they echo in the body of our Earth's wild interior—no place, assuredly, for cherubim or heraldic water birds—heading north, perhaps, following the crease in the palm, or down along the "lifeline" south, resting with Buddhas and lime green frogs between unmapped lily pads. Or following the spirit-fire rising through the bright tunnel of the spine, maneuvering the canyons between the eyes, settling unseen amidst the islands rising from the dark sea behind the brow, raising their plumage like antennae to the moon's warm wind, rustling night-blooming jasmine through their shining feathers.

As a boy, I sat in my canoe on the mirror waters of Lake Winnipesaukee and watched the loons slide and drop beneath the sky plated on the surface. Looking down through the dark waters to catch a glimpse of their disappearing, my sight trailed off into shadows sliding through the dark, chasing bass and pickerel down through the slippery bottom-grass and rising through the striated light to nest on a floating thatch.

Hummingbirds migrate two hundred and fifty miles across the Sea of Cortez without food or rest on their way to their seasonal home ground—pilgrims headed for the holy land.

Monarchs travel thousands of miles to hang like tropical

flowers from their favorite trees. Salmon swim backward as fingerlings not to be pulled too quickly into the sea, and jump waterfalls when returning to that same hollow in the riverbed from which they wriggled free of their eggs at birth.

The blood that is pumped from our heart to our lungs and back again follows these same migratory routes.

The lightning storms across the surface of the cerebellum presage monsoons toward the equator, and the freezing and thawing of streams and lakes to the north. Flocks of songbirds and butterflies follow the double helix home.

Resting beneath an autumnal oak, my heart readies for its next pilgrimage.

And the loons have headed off to God knows where!

5. WEEPING BULL TEACHINGS

ONE SUNDAY AFTERNOON, in my 1964 drug bardo*, misled by the braggadocio of old ghosts, I attended the bull-ring three blocks from my home just outside Mexico City.

There was nothing heroic there.

After two "brave" bulls had been ceremoniously slaughtered, the torero doors swung open and the third sacrifice entered the ring. He did not charge out snorting and bucking,

---

* In the Tibetan Book of the Dead, a *bardo* is sometimes designated as an interstice between lives.

as had the others. He was shoved reluctantly into the ring. It did not want to fight. He ran from the matador. He bellowed and pled. He was not a death-black, square-shouldered, fighting bull, but a brown steer that looked like someone had sold their pet 4-H project to the wrong *vaquero*. The "bull" was terrified and ran around and around the ring. When the picadors pierced its hide, it shrieked for help. The matador was young and flustered and missed several passes, only further wounding and terrifying the animal that ran about, looking for escape.

After many failed passes by the clearly disturbed matador, the crowd, horrified by this blatantly unheroic scene, went mad. The crowd began to stomp and yell, "*Mata lo, mata lo*"— *Kill it, kill it*—again and again as the poor animal wailed in terror. *Mata lo! Mata lo! Mata lo!* A compassionate rage vibrated the blood-spattered walls of the *torero*.

At last, with an awful bellow from the steer and an anguished wail from the audience, the "bull" was killed as dead as Lorca at the firing wall or *Dominguina a las cinco de la tarde*.

We experienced compassion and rage in the same moment. The crowd was on its feet shouting at the inexperienced matador. There was even a sense of danger to the matador, a feeling that at any moment someone might spontaneously jump into the bullring as *novicieros* occasionally do to prove their courage, but this time to dispatch the matador and save the bull. People were stamping their feet in outrage: *Kill it, kill it, have mercy, kill it!*

I knew that bull. At that time, I too felt the frightened hope for escape. The teaching did not elude me. In the face of suffering, help is needed! Another moment that draws us toward the One.

PART 1: YOUTH

Not the least of the lessons from the animal spirits came from that terrible moment with the bull.

Indeed, years later, I thought back to that poor animal's awful death as a profound teaching in mercy and euthanasia. Particularly when I heard a respected religious teacher say that his cosmological fantasy insisted that one must, at the end of one's life, continue suffering, no matter how great the torment. He used as confirmation of such rigid mercilessness a quotation from distant scripture that even a broken-backed old horse dying in agony in the gutter with a crow pecking at its eyes should not be aided in its death.

Many, fearing the loss of a heaven they long ago felt they were unworthy of, have somehow equated suffering with holiness. Not having resolved their personal guilt and grief, they still believe they deserve to suffer. And they deny mercy to themselves and the world of pain that is so worthy of compassion, and calling out for surcease.

Part 2

———

THE CABIN

6. THE SALAMANDER OF FORGIVENESS

I MADE MY WAY UP THE MOUNTAIN in the rain, coming to the cabin in the redwoods, soaked to the bone with grief.

The hinge was slow to relent, the hearth cold and unwilling. An old green chair was full of dusty mice. The nibbled remnants of early maps lay by the chair. The first thing to do in the morning was to find a spot where the sun was leaning over the high redwoods and would remain on the forest floor more than four hours, and prepare a garden.

I had not planted a garden since I was a child before I became "lost in the dark wood of the world," but the Earth remembered me, welcomed me, put her arms around me and let me weep on my knees with seed and trowel on the dark soil.

For years, I lost touch with the planet, and eventually with myself. Having left the fields and woods of my youth, already pitted with restlessness and in search of the origin of this confusion, I lived in the city and followed many paths. Some led to considerable pain, some approached grace. For years, I had no animals around me. I was all too human. But when the world had eaten my head sufficiently, I went back to the quiet of the tall trees.

Each morning, when I lived in the isolated cabin in the redwoods during a very difficult time in my life, I went for a walk in the woods and sat by a small pond in a clearing about a mile away. Divorced. Separated from my children, except for weekends. Homeless in so many ways. My spiritual practice at the bottom of a broken cup. A pain in my chest pulling on my brow.

I wandered through the redwood regrowth, around the labor train full of Chinese laborers and Sharpei work dogs that was buried in the 1906 earthquake. Sometimes, walking, if you stop and put your ear to the ground, you might hear them singing, and their prayers for the wellbeing of all might wick up through the soil. Particularly ornate heavens are their temporary home. Giant Redwood Asuras guard them. A huge, rusted saw-wheel, which has not cut a bleeding giant in a century, stands upright on a ledge where the wind can harp through its tines.

One day, a few months into my daily round of the transfusions of reading, meditating as best I could, Bach and Elton John, and just sitting in the deep forest and letting it heal me, I met a salamander, a near-extinct one at that. Nothing senses time like extinction. I presume endangered species are a bit more psychic than most.

My mind and body became as still as the surrounding forest, as I watched with rapt attention, for perhaps half an hour, the glistening salamander walking methodically across my sneaker. It would take a few steps, then do a few push-ups and head north an inch or so, then turn and head recklessly for the tread that signaled the edge of the world, at the last instant recognizing its folly, turning abruptly, and walking slowly back toward the tip of the shoe and the mossy log from which he had originally stepped onto the sneaker. This moment-to-moment attention to its every movement and twitch, its tiny nails scraping, its eyes blinking and half-blinking, brought my mind back together into one piece. I was fascinated with the sunlight reflecting off each of its prismatic muscular ripples. It took the salamander's slowly undulating backbone a whole lifetime to cross my foot.

And something within, as though it had been forever hiding its countenance, turned toward me and said, "Stephen, I love you." I felt as though I had been struck in the chest, I could barely catch my breath. It spoke of love in the voice I had been waiting to hear my whole life: my own voice. The only voice in which I might have believed it.

And then it, or something, said, "You are forgiven for everything you have ever done!" The salamander stopped in a bit of dappled sunlight. "Oh, but that can't be, there is so much," I said. To which the voice fervently replied, "It's all done now! If you want to pick it up again, that's up to you." I could see how strongly my negative attachment drew me almost compulsively to reach back into the fire to keep punishing myself.

And I knew right then that if I could forgive myself, I could forgive anyone.

One of the hardest processes I have ever experienced was to let myself be forgiven.

7. SPIDERS

SPIDERS CRAWL THE WALLS of the mind; we attempt to stay away from the edge. Making friends with spiders can be an important step in self-discovery. The spider is a mirror for the trembling of the Id, an eight-legged Shiva juggling our primal fears with the wisdom that lays just beyond.

No one ever told me spiders were worth knowing. Actually, even in later life, while learning with the Buddhist Sangha, every once in a while, even from an esteemed teacher, could be heard a dislike of insects in general and an unmistakable imbalance toward, even dread of spiders. For some, it seems spiders rank just below sharks and snakes and just above the lower order of demons. Even granddaddies on stilts make us flinch; their eight legs tightrope the edge of fear. Dread, the mindless turning away, increases their tonnage considerably, but if we have a willingness to "use" the moment, to experience a turning toward, then we receive a rich learning from our fear, which, like those eight ballerina slippers on the near-weightless Daddy Long Legs, can tickle us with delight.

My first spider, and probably the dozen I met afterward, were summarily dispatched. Wet spots. No blame, and the dreadful empowerment of ignorant cruelty.

In the cabin in the redwoods, I slept in a rough-hewn but very comfortable loft. The roof slanting above the mattress, its boards long since shrunk to display between them the planks that held the tarpaper shingles on the roof. Between my striated ceiling and the old redwood slabs that roofed us was a considerable colony of gray and maroon spiders. When I laid on my back, I could watch their daily commerce and what seemed to be their connubial scamperings about a foot above my face. When I had first come to the cabin, exploring my new habitat, the spiders had soon come into view. I slept on an old couch downstairs for the first ten days or so. But settling into a new life, rediscovering our flying spirit—the dragon of the interstice on whose back we are assured we will be carried to our next evolutionary step—we put our feet in the stirrups and with whatever small voice can be mustered say *onward* and take the leap. I moved up to the loft.

Looking up into the spider world, I had to at least attempt some level of compromise. Meditating on their wellbeing, in order to, perhaps, at least not threaten them with my presence, I proposed a working relationship, reminding them that if they dropped onto the bed while I was sleeping they might be crushed by sleep's turnings, which I did not want to do for both our sakes. And promising that I would do nothing intentionally to harm them in any way, with insecticides or swatters, to even be protective of the lifestyle they had developed in the years the cabin was not occupied.

And for this, I received no surprise visits and in general an acknowledgement of territories: They stayed in the roof and I stayed on the floor. Now, absurd as this may seem, in the many months I lived in the cabin, before meeting the salamander and later riding the mouse down the mountain, not one of the hundreds of spiders dropped onto me while I slept. Indeed, I never even found one on my bed or ever again in the room below. Do spiders have Buddha Nature or are they just sensitive to the feelings of others, as any hated innocent might be?

This experiment in consciousness opened further my relationship with the spiders of fear and the spiders of wonderment who crawl over our forearm, stop to pray, and disappear a bit more lovingly into the underbrush of the mind. It was a meditation on everything from the fear of death and injury to a sense of gratitude for being honored to live so closely to the invisible world that lives around us forever. It was a full plate of sweet and sour, love and fear, of the nature of the world around and within me.

I had a somewhat similar spider teaching while I was leading a meditation retreat in the Austin meditation center outside Houston. In the wet lowland where the facility was located, it could be noticed throughout the new, well-made house that spiders were starting to colonize one open ceiling in much the same way as my "red jumpers," as they were referred to. On the third day of the five-day retreat, ten inches of rain fell overnight, flooding the retreatants' tents and campsites. And uprooted as well were the hundreds of spiders that inhabited the brush along the small stream. The spiders were looking for any dry spot in which to survive. The main meeting tent was sopping wet. Some meditators "playing the edge" continued to practice nonetheless. The spiders were climbing up the tent poles, the mic stand and podium, and across the laps and the shoulders of several meditators. Although there was a frightened exquisiteness to the whole gestalt, we said, "Meditation called off on account of spiders!" Some were disappointed, others all too glad to get to safe territory. Bitten though we certainly would have been, I can see the value of us all having stuck with it, softening with loving kindness to even that which assaults us, and inviting Gandhi to show us not just the never-passive resistance but also the non-injury that is the heart of Satyagraha (and was the soul of the political movement) to free all that is captive within and around us. To loose the grip of the demon-kind that is projected upon all we fear and would destroy. It's just a spider.

The cricket, the wasp, the moth, and especially the scarab beetle have found their way into innumerable metaphorical tales in many religions. Even Kafka turned cockroach. The Chinese inventor of paper, Cai Lun (48–121AD), according to legend, was shown the process of wasps making their nests by chewing tree bark and mixing it with their saliva. The spider, lauded for its patience, is immortalized on the Nasca plain in Peru.

One day, as I was speaking in the sanctuary with a visiting ornithologist from the University of Arizona, on the adobe wall behind him rose a wolf spider a good deal larger than my hand. It reminded me of some of the water spiders we used to encounter in Winnipesaukee when we dove over the gunnels to catch a water snake. I noted much less fear of the snake I knew, which had bitten me harmlessly on various occasions, than of the hairy floater that I didn't know. The spider on the wall unwarily behind the ornithologist, I was sure was not his favorite, as it at times ate small birds. And, if startled, I knew he might instinctively swat it with the book he had in hand. But this was a sanctuary and there would be no killing here. So I invited him onto the porch, watching the marsh hawk hover over the cienega-marsh and excused myself for a minute to take care of "wolfie-baby." When I noticed the primal stutter-step of fear I softened my hands so that fear would not be communicated, placed a shoe box over the walled spider, and carried it back to the teeming marsh.

8. THE MOUSE OF FAITH

JUST AS THE SALAMANDER of forgiveness had brought me back to the present, I knew I could use a little help returning to a noisy, angry, self-hating world, to "come off the mountain," figuratively and actually.

And once again, the right books appeared at just the right time.

In one, a Chinese fable told how each person must choose an animal spirit capable of supporting and conveying his or her constantly expanding spirit body. Some used a bull or a workhorse, others an elephant or a whale or even a dragon. Some of the most wily chose a fox, or while herding, an ox.

But as I looked about in the woods and in my mind for a suitable conveyance for my undernourished spirit body, only the small gray mouse, hopping from sunspot to sunspot across the weathered wooden planks of the porch, seemed to wholly comprehend the potential for boundless fear or boundless joy.

And I took the mouse to heart.

It suggested further reading of my old friend Ram Dass's new book in particular, recently received as an artful conglomeration in a box from the Lama Foundation—where seven years later, Ondrea and I would meet, and three years after that, Ram Dass would marry us.

The name of the work that initiatory week in 1973 was *Be Here Now*. It reminded me there was so much more to the world than pain. Page after page of the book cut my old moorings and drew me out to sea. Across the horizon through the great heart of Ram Dass and into the arms of his enormous teacher, Neem Karoli Baba, known affectionately and respectfully as Maharaji (often translated Great King or, better yet in this case, Great Spirit).

And the mouse grew stronger.

Taking one breath at a time, I began to find my way back out of the past into the present. But it was a very different present than I had known. I was not alone. Tiny scythes scampered across the stone floor of forgetfulness to remind me.

And the mouse of faith carried me down the mountain through the redwood regrowth, around the labor train buried full of Chinese laborers and Sharpei work dogs after the 1906 earthquake. Riding down the hill, I could hear their muttered prayers wicking up through the soil. Ornate heavens were their temporary home. Giant redwood Asuras guarded them. The huge rusted saw-wheel, which had not cut a bleeding giant in a century, stood upright on a ledge where the wind could harp through its tines, and the mouse called the Earth to witness.

Part 3

SANCTUARY

9. ENTERING SANCTUARY

W HEN I FIRST MET MY TEACHERS—
Rudi and Ram Dass, Elizabeth
Kubler-Ross and the Dalai Lama—there
was a deep intoning. Something in me wanted to touch my forehead to their feet. I knew
we had work together.

But before I could do that, I had to touch the Earth, to
"bring the Earth to witness" as they said of the Buddha's touching the ground to dispel the distractions that were assailing
him. There are many initiations along the way to becoming a
whole human being, but first and last are our connection with
the Earth and animal spirits.

Finding my place in the food chain, I tended the Canelo
Hills Wildlife Sanctuary (also called the Canelo Hills Cienega)
in southern Arizona for The Nature Conservancy. I had a horse,
a badge, and a typewriter.

* * *

In the spring of 1970, I repeatedly sat with the feelings of frus-
tration so many were voicing about the lack of protection of this
magical green globe we float upon. There was an ache in the
heart for all that is being lost of forest, stream, salamander, butterfly, whale, agave, petroglyphed outcropping, the panther's

spirit ascending Mount Kilimanjaro, every three-legged frog, every kingfisher panting on its side dying of pesticides beside a poisoned stream, all the lifeless rivers, along with all our brothers and sisters being flogged into starvation in Africa, all our brothers and sisters sweating their lives out on AIDS-soaked sheets, all our sisters and brothers losing their lives day by day to prejudice and fear, to cold indifference, and all that suffer and die in man and nature, in the very nature of man, despite our love. I cannot help but weep when I think of it all.

Allen Cohen, my old partner at the *San Francisco Oracle,* suggested one day I call this fellow he had met who worked for The Nature Conservancy and ask him about the possibility of my tending one of their wilderness preserves.

I was hired and offered a wildlife sanctuary to tend in southern Arizona. The only water for miles around was an underground stream that surfaced for just a mile or so and then returned to its cool underground chambers. It was a riparian Eden, with a hundred and twenty-five species of birds, at the northernmost migratory range for some South American species and the southernmost range for a number of northern birds. There were coatimundi, javelina, coyote, pronghorn, and all the furry fellows one might imagine would be drawn to such a wet spot in the midst of a high desert savanna.

* * *

THE GREAT EARTH SPIRIT OF GRANNO KNIPE

Two months before The Nature Conservancy acquired the Canelo Hills Sanctuary, the Knipe clan congregated to decide what was to become of the family homestead, which had been empty for years since Grandma Knipe, who everyone called Granno, had passed on. For three decades, Granno had lived alone in the old adobe house. The neighbors, a bit peeved that she was not interested in their company, said she was "eccentric." But Granno just didn't want people on the land; "It disturbs the animals," she said.

Granno had felt the spirit of the land, and spoken to the ancient chiefs that had long since passed from the hills and had the deer eating from her deeply creased palm the native grains and fresh sweet corn she grew for them alone. She had found her place watching skunks dance in a circle in the moonlight, talking to the old brown bear, or winking at the bobcat scuttling into his rocky den beneath the spreading roots of the great oak beyond the stream, more afraid of the sun than Granno's good morning salute. It was Granno who drew throughout the house the symbols of the Hohokam, the canal-building agricultural Indians of eight hundred years before, who first cultivated this land and left it whole for their descendants, the Pueblo and Papago. Hohokam frescoes drawn along either side of the fireplace directed the smoke toward heaven. On the weathered exterior wall of the porch, she had incised in a mandala the lizard and lightning signs of the Hohokam's integration of earth and heaven.

Granno's presence was everywhere, particularly about the house where she had spent her last thirty years watching the seasons and speaking with the animals. It was Granno who first consecrated this land; it was her attitude which was the predecessor of sanctuary.

* * *

As a sanctuary guide, the best I can do is to be an usher accompanying each scientist and ecologist to the species of their greatest interest. Ornithologists, I take to see the small green heron or the painted redstart. Reptilian biologists, I introduce to the rare rock rattler or the disappearing tail of a Sonoran whip snake, or perhaps indicate with a passing pat on the head a puppy-like horned toad along the path. With ichthyologists, I get lazy by the stream, watching the dace knit shadows to the shore as my friend the catostomus plows the dark depths. Or with a geologist, I go walking to the bottom of the deep arroyo, with its walls rising fifteen feet to ground level, striated with previous cienegas and plains, like cross-section rings in a tree chronicling fifty thousand years of accumulated growth. It all makes me realize that the whole planet is girdled by these rings, strata of soil built up since prehistory, and that the planet itself is the tree of life on which we grow.

10. THE HUMMINGBIRD WAR: A BENEDICTION

VISITING WITH THE MELLORS, who helped us acclimate here and introduced us to the far-flung community of cowboys and ranchers, we sat at their ranch house table, talking about the thick-billed parrot which once migrated to the Huachuca Mountains. Speaking of the food that each habitat must provide for a creature to remain there, Cassie Mellor said, "Oh, that reminds me, I've let the six hummingbird feeders go empty. Would you refill them for me?" She had always allowed at least one feeder to be full of the red nectar the hummingbirds had come to expect after so many years. The black-chinned and broad-billed hummingbirds returning from migration had just buzzed the window to remind us all of our duty.

Taking the gallon jug of hummingbird food from the refrigerator and the twelve-foot aluminum ladder from behind the house, I came around to the living room window, where the row of feeders pointed an empty, accusing finger. A black-chinned hummingbird, who was among the first to return, feeling he should be first to partake of the afternoon repast, sat on the broad lid to the jug as I climbed the ladder. Taking down the small inverted bottles from their wire hangers, I started to fill the first bottle as an iridescent broadtail on his way up the Huachucas came closer, trying to see exactly what was happening, then backed off a few inches as another came buzzing in to sip from the bottle still in my hand.

And the word was out.

From nests as delicate as spiderwebs, the hummingbirds appeared as though from out of nowhere while I poured from the great jar of Kool-Aid-like hummingbird goody. The black-chinned bird, who had ridden up the ladder with me, poked his head down into the wide-mouth gallon jug. And soon all about me were dozens of hummingbirds, spinning and whizzing. They made a planetarium of action: antimatter spinning through black holes in space and materializing again; coming up under my arm, across my ear, onto my shoulder, my forearm; sitting on my head; their buzzing, whirring, super-sonic wings spinning in that unique rotary motion that allows their angular descent and amazing rises through space. I could no sooner fill one bottle and hang it up than hummers would be sitting on my fingers sipping, waiting for me to release the bottle so that they might drink more. One broad-bill perched incredibly on my nose, looking straight into my eyes like a fly pressed against a spaceship window—so much for us to see in each other's reality. Then came the softest sensation I have ever experienced in nature: a ruby throat sitting on my forearm, whirring and sizzling, feeling like petals opening from a flower growing out of roots anchored in my nervous system, my nerve ends fluttering out, indistinguishable from the sizzling hum of these tiny birds chattering to each other that a delightful red dessert was being served.

Twelve feet up on the aluminum ladder—surrounded by hummingbirds, my shoulders decorated with perched feath-ered epaulets, at my wrists hanging from the corner of my shirt fine iridescent cufflinks, tiny and full of life, like electrons whir-ring through molecular space seeking their haven—I felt like a nursing boar, my offspring two dozen whizzing hummers, my breasts those six jars filled with sugar and red food coloring, my teats those long glass tubes reflected in the window before me. There could be nothing simultaneously gentler or more violent than two hummingbirds mating, nothing more delicate or more like the collision of planets in space.

11. KARMAPA'S HORSE

THERE ARE SAID TO BE legendary enlightened beings who have undertaken
to work on the behalf of all sentient beings
until all the realms of pain and confusion
have been emptied. These enlightened beings
include the Karmapas, who were known for their ability to
teach animals, and could, it was rumored, assume the form of
marvelous beasts.

I had not yet met the Dalai Lama when I was invited to
a large gathering for the Karmapa who was visiting a local Tibetan Buddhist study group. (The Dalai Lama and the
Karmapa are considered the very highest manifestations of
Chenrezi, the energy holder of the Great Compassion.) I stood
in line with hundreds of others for most of a Sunday afternoon
to receive the Karmapa's blessing.

Standing in line, I was reminded of the stories of Karmapa's
love for animals, particularly birds, and of his legendary horse
who, it was said, gave blessings by placing one of its hooves
on a person's head. People would wait in line, waiting for their
turn to be blessed, and as the horse touched their head, it was
known to sound the seed syllable *hum*.

Most people got touched very lightly, but once in a while
someone got whacked hard.

Some people were reticent to ask for a blessing that might
crack open their head but many more heard in the touch the

heart song *om mani padme hum*, literally straight from the horse's mouth. One fellow who stood in such a line recalled "I thought to myself, 'Who knows what that horse will do to me? Maybe it will split my skull open!'"

After being blessed, I sat in the large hall, reflecting on what, if any, energy had been transmitted to me in the momentary touch of one of the great Buddhist living masters. I accepted the slightly disappointing low-key ritual of a meet-and-greet with the Karmapa. It left no hoof print on me. It was nice, but not worth missing the Superbowl for, as the saying goes. I was still not enlightened.

I was about to leave when one of the members of the meditation group whom the Karmapa would be visiting next invited me to join the gathering because I was a local Buddhist meditation teacher, though of a different school.

I was told to stay respectfully back as the Karmapa passed through the room with his retinue of monks, and to stand behind the two rows of Vajrayana practitioners who had originally invited him to the Santa Cruz Sangha. I stood wondering to myself if such a remarkable teacher could give me some insight into the work I was doing and the manner in which I was employing Buddhist meditation techniques to aid the dying. I was concentrating on this question as he came toward me down the line of avid mediators, stopped at the people in front of me, and, reaching between them, *whacked!* my shoulder with a very powerful blessing. It was a proverbial pat on the shoulder, except it was from the Buddha. It was a blessing that still resonates in my bones thirty years later.

It has been said that one day the Karmapa's horse just sat down on its hindquarters and passed away, then continued sitting there without any signs of decay, in the manner of an enlightened being.

* * *

It was part of my job at the sanctuary to ride up imposingly on my horse to the poachers. My horse, Duster, was a beautiful mare we had bought from a neighbor's son. She hated to cross streams, and had to back up a few steps and jump over even the merest trickle, so we had to approach some of the poachers sideways when they were across the stream, which became a joke between Duster and me. When I reached the poachers, after having flashed my badge, which was actually an emblem patch on my shirt, I would tell them this was protected land and they would have to go elsewhere. But on one occasion, I heard shots ring out from a thousand yards away and by the time I got there, a doe lay dying as the hunters ran off. Sitting with that dying friend as she bled out, as the world bled out, as the heart we all share emptied like a broken bucket, a silence enveloped us. I tried to match my breathing with the doe's: the inbreath hard and pained, then slowing, and the outbreath stuttering and stopping, with the doe coughing up some blood as the breath was released out into the unbroken blue sky.

Clearly, the work we do on ourselves is for the benefit of all sentient beings.

And so Duster and I would ride slowly along the fence, watching the birds and beasts find their niche away from the eyes of man and horse alike. Her sorrel filly, who we named Cienega after this rich marsh, frolicked behind us, passed us, scooted about in circles and back again, kicking the wind beside us as I was graced to sit astride the broad back of Duster.

One late afternoon, I escaped up to the mesa on Duster, and as we rounded the edge of the hill, we broke into a full gallop, yodeling peace cries to the wide sky. And for the first time I experienced "the silver field"—the sensory experience of horse and rider as one, our motion interwoven, riding, riding, a centaur at last!

As I galloped the great mesa behind the old frontier adobe with Duster leaning into the wind, I got some sense of the oneness between animal and human that the North American tribal peoples so lauded. And sensing the fine-edged combining of the elements of wind and fire, earth and sweat, sometimes I would let go of my fear of running full-out into the vicinity of the prairie dogs and I would let the Great Spirit guide our path.

Surrendering in the saddle with your hair blowing back, on the verge of impermanence, is a little different than surrendering on your quiet meditation pillow. That mesa had a lot to teach me, and Duster was one of my guru sisters on the journey. She knew which way to turn before I did. Because she would jump rather than step through even a shallow stream, she taught me a bit about the steeple chase as well. She had a great heart.

We bought Duster the quarter-horse mare with her air-kicking one-month-old filly tagging along—Duster was a nine-year-old cow pony raised as a 4-H project by one of the Mellors' sons, and her filly was thrown in like a spare tire. Through Duster, we soon came to appreciate the ability and willing strength of the quarter-horse, those "gutsy four-square horses" who, in Colonial times were bred from Chickasaw Indian mares and English-blooded stallions.

We brought her home and watched her lightning mane flowing in the wind as she ran the length of the cienega, a living image of freedom.

Riding the fence now myself, experiencing the autumn of my life, I ask myself, *Who can own another's flesh?* Yet we have bought horses. To own something is to be responsible for it: to fit into it, finding your place within, your valence for it, being responsible for yourself in it. To own a horse is to own a life, to get upon another's back and tell them where you wish to go.

To own a horse, a living creature, is akin to imagining one can own land, a piece of the living planet. The county clerk is not a holy herald, and cannot convey the Earth's corpuscles or describe the mineral genealogy of a grazing pronghorn. The native peoples knew they could not own the land because they could not control it. Man, in his present delusion imagines that he can master the land and therefore own it, but it is not so: he and the land erode in constant proportion to the other's lack of native freedom. A horse, like a piece of land, responds in direct proportion to the respect and kindness it is offered. Each willingly offers its energies in response to love.

For me, purchasing a horse was much like planting a garden. There was a need to tend the wellbeing of the organism before any sustenance could be requested. I had ridden only a few times in my life, but always on undisciplined ponies in an undisciplined manner.

But this was different; the introduction of a horse into my life was a dramatic change in technology. It allowed me to become one of the shadows in the oak forest, to approach other animals with a very different gait and smell, to sit quietly at the edge of the meadow beneath an antique mulberry and feel the wings of thrushes and buntings brush by me into the lattice-work of branches, an iridescent ounce of cytoplasm up into the crown of the tree.

The introduction of the horse changed Amerindian society as not even the introduction of electricity affected ours. No single alteration in technology has ever caused as radical a change in the consciousness of a people as did the coming of the horse, and I can see why.

The lifestyle changes of many tribal peoples are recorded in their pictographic and storytelling arts and might easily be dated B.H. and A.H.: Before Horse and After Horse.

To the Amerindians, the horse was a vision come true, an element leaked from the Other World, the fourth world, the real world, of which we are only shadows.

* * *

NOVEMBER

Sitting at the breakfast table this morning, I looked out across the marsh to see the filly dashing back and forth along the riparian tree line. The filly was very excited, but her mother was nowhere to be seen. Crossing the marsh quickly, she led us to her mother, who lay half-dead in the stream.

For some reason, Duster had entered the creek during the night, stepping into a deep water pocket, moving downstream, ducking a fallen tree and coming up again with her head caught in the fork of a limb, unable to escape, the cold waters numbing her. We found her lying with her head against the dark mud bank, unable to move. Up to my ribs in winter's freezing stream, I held the chainsaw like a scalpel very close to her neck, removing the fallen tree limb. Duster's hind legs were hardly able to support her as I coaxed her further downstream to shallower water and up a gentle bank, then ever so slowly across the cienega toward the corral. By the time we arrived, both of us were exhausted and numb; then it was time for barley and the deep warmth of molasses, and good morning.

* * *

THANKSGIVING BLESSING—
FULL MOON, LAST DAY OF DEER SEASON.

I become extinct like buffalo and bald eagle.
Dinosaur was around for one hundred and fifty million
years
then couldn't make it anymore.
We've been here just a million and already
we threaten to take all else with us.

Part 4

LEARNING TO SEE

12. THE EYE OF BEAUTY

W HAT WOULD IT BE LIKE to open our eyes and actually see the beauty around us? To look around us at a world more beautiful than we ever conceived. To see into a world of possibilities beneath the one our senses have been ricocheting off through most of our lives. To appreciate how light dissipates shadow on the surface of that which has long been taken for granted. To listen to what we have previously only heard as it passed in one ear and out the other.

On days when we wake to the wonder of things, there arises the unimagined possibility of what the mind trembles to acknowledge as love.

When the heart opens, the Eye of Beauty opens. And we begin to see "the hidden art" everywhere, the "grand picture" in the details.

We see the design of the universe, the whole of physics in the swirls of a seashell. The constellations within a fleck of mica. The moon reflected in a droplet of water at the tip of a leaf. The sunlight in a single falling snowflake. The evolution of the species in the high notes of a thrush. The macrocosm in the microcosm. The Everything in everything.

Repositioning our focus opens the Eye of Beauty. The art inside the painting is in the brushstrokes on the canvas. The rising up of the Himalayas in a rocky overhang. The face of the Beloved in a weather-pitted outcropping.

The sources of beauty are not in the light but in the luminescence within. When we recognize the light behind the shadow-play of consciousness, the wisdom eye, the Eye of Beauty sees clearly.

The Eye of Beauty looks into the ripples in the petals of flowers, not just at their color but at the play of Monet's light; at the canyons echoing with all the lives that have passed by in furrowed bark like the creasing in the corners of the eyes. The topographic map of a life long-lived in the wrinkles of the aged. The Mondrians in the fractured ice.

Seeing past the images-of-old imprinted on the single layer of cells at the surface of the cerebellum. Crossing the connection between the hemispheres. Seeing the art in nature, the forgotten architecture.

There, beneath the thread-bare preconceptions of what we ordinarily see, is what *is to be seen*. Ordinarily, all that we see is what we have previously seen. We rarely see *the flower*, we only see a flower. It is not the world that becomes old but the cipher between the eye and the mind, between what we think we see and what we are actually seeing.

To observe directly—to look with the Eye of Beauty—is to live from the heart. We see from the absolute present, rather than the drowsy past, practicing mindfulness and loving kindness toward all sentient beings—including even so unlikely a candidate as oneself. Mercy breaks all the rules.

The Eye of Beauty sees from the open heart. It sees from love. It is a love not unlike the beauty revealed to the fresh eye of one newly in love. When we are freshly in love, nothing has changed but our point of view. The ordinary is new. The world at such moments is indescribably beautiful.

There are innumerable stories about those who fell in love in the most trying times, even during wartime, and still found the world so very precious because of the presence of their beloved. Love at its zenith can be stronger than our fear of death.

The Eye of Beauty sees what lies beneath the unholy suffering we fear we will find if we go deeper. But when we go deeper yet, we find a beauty beyond our wildest dreams, the essential grace of our enormity.

13. THE WHEEL OF EXISTENCE

AT THE HUB OF THE WHEEL OF EXISTENCE are the symbolic animals. The pig, which will eat almost anything, stands for desire; the serpent stands for anger; and the rooster, which will crow even at a bright moon and still runs around even with its head cut off, is characteristic of ignorance or delusion.

The Buddhist teacher Shantideva said that tigers, lions, elephants, bears, and serpents reside in the mind as the various emotions. He suggested we quiet the jungle of the mind with the "great gestures" of gratitude, kindness, sympathetic joy, and loving kindness.

The pain of our longing for peace drives us to *find our sit* and occupy it, to close our eyes, to let the eyes soften behind closed

lids, to let the breath breathe itself, to let go of the holding-in
the belly, softening with each in-breath, softening the breath,
the pain that councils us to draw near the illumination coming
from the heart. Longing is the pain that ends pain, and it is
actually the pain that ends suffering.

14. THE PRAIRIE DOGS AND THE ASCENDED LAMAS

W HEN WE LIVED IN TAOS, behind our
small adobe home were a couple of
hundred acres of what became a prairie dog
community. Each morning the scamper and
chatter of the village told us of the new births
and the fading and deaths of the populace, and how cold it was
last night. In the high mountains of the Southwest, the winter
nights are often below freezing even though the days may well
be seventy degrees on the sunny mound on which the prairie
dogs busy themselves.

During the coldest, twenty-degrees-below-zero weeks in
January, I wondered how they could survive, and was told that
the prairie dog has the remarkable facility of suspended ani-
mation, their metabolism almost completely closing down so
that crystals can actually form in their blood with no detriment
to the animal.

When I heard this, it reminded me of experiencing the
delightful clarity of the highly-regarded Tibetan monk Lama

Yeshe as he was reviewing for me a guided meditation for the dying that I was working on, based somewhat on the *Tibetan Book of the Dead*. At one point, I asked him how it was possible for some very advanced monk-practitioners to apparently die, all of their life functions seemingly closed down, yet remain sitting erect and without the least deterioration or decay for weeks in the chair in which they had died. Presumably, this occurred so they could stay in close working relationship to the Dharmata, the great light of our great nature, which appears to most relatively briefly after they die. The Dharmata is the great door through which it is the chance of a lifetime to pass into the boundlessness of Being. *If the monks have that much power and control as to stay one element of death,* I asked, *why could they not just merge with it completely as is the stated goal?* To which Lama Yeshe replied—and this may give some elucidation to the Buddha remarking that it takes "eons" to reach the goal wholeheartedly and without end— that even for the advanced meditator, "It's not as easy as you think!"

Prairie dogs remain suspended between life and death through the long night in their dark burrows; Lamas remain suspended between life and death in the sunrise through the bright tunnel.

* * *

Our hundred-year-old frontier adobe house had slits rather than windows on its back, and faced a rising mesa. (The slits, we were told, were for rifles during Apache raids.) We welcomed the long rocky plateau into our sanctuary. We often explored the mesa's sides, draws, arroyos, and the lip of the butte, and, of course, we rode the long tabletop plain.

One of the most exquisite teachings from the mesa took place when I got lost miles into a rapt exploration of the spring wildflowers and scampering hatchlings. While walking with a Japanese "hidden bodhisattva" friend on the mesa, we headed off toward a distant rocky outcropping. Walking and talking, and not talking, we walked the base of the rock formation, noting where the tribal peoples had sat and struck arrowheads, mostly out of raw, recently-traded obsidian; clips and flakes of shiny beetle-black sharp-edged stone were abundant. There was a turquoise-bellied gecko, transcribing like bejeweled Ganesha, the Glorious Song. And there were pottery shards and stone tools like broken hammers, the usual sturdy mallets, and grinding stones that had been smoothed, cracked in half, and abandoned after years of use.

After spending some time following an ancient animal path back to the tree line, we started to wind our way back along the mesa. But this was an area unfamiliar to me, and it seemed we had walked quite some time before we noticed there were none of the accustomed landmarks. It was getting late in the day and my anxiety began to rise when I realized that we might not make it home before the moonless night, that we could be left wandering. When I told my friend of my perception, that we might become lost, he said, "Don't worry it's such a small planet."

Walking a while toward dusk, I told him that I thought we might be in for a difficult time. To which he smiled that particular Zendo smile and said, "Survival is highly overrated." Softening my belly and surrendering into the silver field, we found our way home in the dark to anxious loved ones awaiting us.

15. FIRE SERMON OF THE ANTS

🐜 **A**TTEMPTING TO ROUSE HIS MONKS to yet greater commitment to practice, the Buddha gave what has come to be known as the Fire Sermon, in which he said that the eyes are on fire, the tongue is on fire, the ears are on fire, the mind is on fire. And he suggested we quench it with the cool stillness of the dharma.

Some years ago, Dharma Benefactor Margaret Austin was in the process of converting a portion of her ranch outside Houston into a meditation facility for the community, and invited Ondrea and me to lead a weekend retreat.

These two-day meditation retreats, which take place in complete silence and mean making a commitment to fifteen to eighteen hours a day of sitting and walking practice, can give one's daily practice quite a boost in concentration and a considerable resurgence of energy.

On the second day, with the participants well settled into the regimen, the group concentration beginning to envelop us during a late afternoon mindfulness walk. Following an old cow path through an open field, I led a few dozen retreatants on a meditation in which each person watches the feet of the person ahead and lifts their own foot as the person in front lifts theirs, and so on, meanwhile being thoroughly submerged in mindfulness of the sensations that accompany each step.

When the practice is done in a circle, one soon realizes that as the person before them is setting their pace, so one is also setting the pace of the person behind. In fact, as one comes to realize, they are all ultimately just following themselves.

Halfway across the pasture, I noticed, in the closely observed field of sensation, a burning in my right calf, as though I had been struck by a metallic spark. Duly noting this new sensation, I continued with another step before multiple fiery insinuations into the open calm of the walking meditation caused me to look less-than-mindfully down to find that I was leading the group through a large nest of fire ants.

As I bravely attempted to "just be mindful" of the stinging assault, I was doing something like the Irish Stomp to shake loose some of the ants now well above the knee. The group did the same. They looked, as they jumped about, raising the red Texas dust, backlit by a huge crimson sun, like red shamans dancing their hearts out to rid this world of confusion. We were all stomping and laughing and yelping bodhisattvas come to wake the Earth, to split it open, to beckon up the Ocean of Compassion. We were drawn kicking and hooting into the fiery center of each bite, into the melted center of the Earth, into the molten heart freed of fear and distrust. We were dancing for our liberation, to free and save us all from that which, rising up, makes us weak in the knees.

16. THE GREED OF CRABS

WHILE AWAITING THE BIRTH of my daughter, I lived across the bay from Haight-Ashbury in a small house that had been built in 1906 to accommodate the outflow of the populace from the San Francisco earthquake. Just down the block from me lived a fellow of unusual sensitivity and humor named Padreco, a retired colonel from the Italian military. We used to tell each other outrageous "fish stories," almost choking on our laughter at the bold mendacity of the three-foot-long scarlet bass who had told Padreco he used to be a Cardinal but slipped on a bottle of wine and fell into the sea where he had lived ever since. Padreco said he kissed the fish, and the next thing he knew, I was ringing his doorbell. I told him that a crab crossing the beach had told me his address and said to go tell him he was a terrible liar.

Sometimes the tears would be rolling down our cheeks as we spent the afternoon fishing for crabs off the Presidio at an old army base beneath the Golden Gate Bridge, lying to each other about the time a Shanghai Crab had shimmied up the catch-line and dragged an Italian prevaricator off the pier and into servitude as a deck mop on a Chilean fishing trawler.

But in the midst of all this good-natured tale-telling, which was something between a T.A.T. (Thematic Apperception Test) and comedy improv, was the oft-repeated, sickening sound of the gulls finding crabs nearby and flying up about thirty feet into the air to drop the crabs onto the rocks below and smash them so they could then swoop down and scoop the soft flesh from their broken bodies. And to add to the dichotomy between our lightheartedness and the ambush of nature, we often felt, when pulling up our nets, that something was amiss with the scene. Clinging to the outside of the closed nets, which contained perhaps a few crabs, were often many more crabs holding onto the outside "for dear life," to be picked by hand off the outside webbing and placed with the more "legitimately caught" into the same bucket.

It seemed such a teaching in the grasping at life, the hanging-on instead of the letting go. Trying to be the perfect crab, one would hold on of his own free will to prove to all the others he didn't need to be captured to look the fisherman in the eye. And, remaining that perfect individual, the crab would be placed in the cooking pot. But on the way out of the pot, it seemed evident that if he had sought liberation instead of myths of perfection, if letting go had been his way into the Ocean of his Being, instead of upholding his incessant perfectionism, he might still be writing children's stories about the light at the bottom of the sea.

This greedy grasping that captures us, this refusing to let go of our impending doom, is acted out by more than just crabs and humans. The monkey hunted in the jungle is often caught by its refusal to release its fateful grasp. Traditionally, when hunting monkeys, people placed narrow-necked gourds containing bananas around the jungle. A voracious monkey would reach down into the narrow neck of the gourd and, grasping a handful of bananas, could not extract its hands without letting go of the food in its fist. Even though the monkey would scream in panic at the approach of the hunter, it still would not release the banana and free itself from its self-imposed trap.

Animals seek perfection as a survival mechanism. Humans are capable of even more: They are capable of liberation. One can be a perfect human or, better yet, a liberated spirit. Perfection entices an individual; liberation includes us all. Perfection is for fishermen who don't know that one can be patient even without waiting. Liberation happens because our heart really wishes for nothing more.

Being born under the astrological sign of Cancer, I am represented by the crab, a sideways-moving creature whose eyes are on stalks in the front of his head. How does he see where he is going? How often does he, driven nonetheless by desire, find himself walking inexplicably away from what he craves. I wonder if the crab is a creature of longing. In the world of spiritual aspiration, it is said that the longing does all the work. Crossing the most contested territory on earth, the intertidal corridor of mollusk breathing holes, tide pools, and the gull's killing fields between low and high tide, the vulnerable crab scurries sideways, its prints leaving runes like musical notes, a song sheet offered into an ocean of singing whales. Has the crab left a pastoral in the long sand prints on the beach? Is he teaching us to read the music that is right there before us?

Someone said the crab walks sideways to display the effect of love on matter. That unique force in nature expands in all directions; without it, nature would not/could not exist.

That which is not unlike love attracts the atom into the molecule. As water turns dirt to clay and clay to vase and vase is offered to kiln or transformed by the sun, that which binds one to another displays its delicate and indestructible essence.

Form is created from formlessness. This is true within and without; indeed, it is the vase's emptiness that predicts its form. This elemental construction of form out of emptiness is the process many spiritual practices attempt to follow back to its source. This attraction to our essential nature, the unconditioned ground of being, the experience of which is unconditional love, seems to be the same in all belief systems. Only the manner of approach appears to be different. Sometimes we meet it head on, sometimes heart first—but, most often, we idle sideways toward the goal.

17. POISON OAK TEACHINGS

T HE TALL TREES CALL US to raise our arms in praise, the underbrush teaches us how to bow.

Clearing brush the evening before a ten-day meditation retreat began, I spattered my arms and face with poison oak. It was not until after the retreat began that its affect was realized.

As my face and arms began to turn red and blister, as an experiment in consciousness, I took a vow not to scratch.

At night, so as not to involuntarily rub it during sleep, I slept with my arms extended above my head like one surrendering. Any movement immediately triggered an alarm. It was the green snake teachings once again!

Before long, my eyes were nearly closed from facial swelling.

At times, when my mindfulness lagged, the compulsion to relieve discomfort started making a very strong case. While on my cushion, my foot would rise off the floor of its own mercy and try to rub my fiery wrist and forearm. I had to just say no.

After a few days, my face and arms were swollen and crusty. In order not to move involuntarily, it was absolutely necessary to maintain moment-to-moment awareness, to stay absolutely present.

My concentration was rarely better.

After a few days of not scratching, just sending mercy into my sizzling skin, my desire for that particular experiment in consciousness was sated. And before my eyes were completely swollen shut, I left the retreat for the afternoon to get a cortisone shot.

Driving to the doctor's office, it seemed to me that the trees were melting. The shafts of sunlight coming through the undulating redwoods were more solid than the liquid road before me. The leaves, the branches, the macadam, the tree trunks, the flowering bushes were all composing and decomposing from moment to moment. It was all a bit like Dali's melting watches. Even my thoughts were unable to stay but an instant before dissolving one into the next. The universe was contracting and expanding ever-anew from millisecond to millisecond. It was an opening of the doors of perception.

Afterwards, it was my sense that perception had expanded from its normal fifteen frames a second to several times that number. Slow-motion seeing was speeding up everything, matter constantly displaying its subatomic restlessness.

Returning a few hours later to my meditation, thankful to the bovine sacrifice which provides cortisone, as I settled in, I noticed that my fascinated seeing had abated. And I heard that big laugh that says, "Even impermanence is impermanent; remember that when you're dying."

Part 5

BELOW RED RIDGE

18. THE LADIES AND THE IN-LAWS

 THIRTY YEARS AGO, Ondrea and I were living in Taos, New Mexico, and "the Ladies" were ensconced quite comfortably in their long, warm chicken coop. They sat in their nests, and the yard was full of the communal clucking of brooding hens and patrolled by the bright avian spark that is a Rhode Island Red rooster.

We raised Rhode Island Reds for the eggs. So the hens would not live in such deplorable conditions, we also adopted a few "egg factory" white Leghorns whose beaks had been clipped short so as to be able to live in severely overcrowded conditions without causing injury to themselves or each other. They had been discarded because they had stopped laying. Where their beaks had been trimmed, they continued to grow into what resembled collagened lips—they were sad Leghorns with Betty Boop lips. After about a month of proper feeding and nesting space, they began to lay again. Their eggs were golden. The Ladies ran through our raised garden beds, and were often seen chasing a grasshopper at full speed across the field in front of the house.

Among the colorful clutch of Polish Golden, Araucana, Light Sussex, Maran, and Plymouth Rock hens was one particularly large Rhode Island Red we called Big Red. Most chickens scatter when another chicken walks through a group, but Big Red used to squat down and make herself a bit wider so that one would not pass her by without giving her a pet on her soft clucking back.

Once, when we were unexpectedly visited by a high Tibetan Lama, a Tulku, while I was preparing supper, I asked him if he would care to share in the meal I was preparing, hesitantly adding that we were having chicken for supper, which I did not know was acceptable to his practice. Noting my discomfort, he laughed and said, "Yes, chicken please. You know, I do chicken great favor. I turn chicken into Lama."

* * *

Eggs were stirring in the incubator and all was right with the world.

I don't think I even noticed the first one, the first world, that is: the one we are born into, which our needs split apart like it's too small a skin shed. It landed unnoticed.

One day, a lone homing pigeon fluttered into the chicken yard. I saw her doing a little sand-shoe dance, but never thought that her friends and relatives might be on the way. I had forgotten that, like bees, birds dance to map the way to new food sources. To make a long story short, that single pigeon became about forty in the next weeks, all of them inhabiting the large coop, eating enough of the chickens' cracked corn to create ethanol to heat their plump little bodies and make flight fuel. Many varieties of homing and European rock doves, along with the overbearing King pigeon and a few other natty dressers, like magpies, dropped by to mingle with the growing herd. And squirrels and skunks came in as the night janitors, and rabbits peered through the fencing.

In the coop was the sound of heaven. Entering, we were surrounded, lifted into the pure cacophony, the soul music of dozens of chickens murmuring and scores more of the squatter pigeons in chorale.

When we moved from Taos up into the mountain woodlands, with the chickens in tow, the coyotes began to survey the menu from behind an oak shrub or a well-lichened boulder, waiting for their chance. A year or so into our new digs, the free-ranging flock was getting thinned and the chickens had to go back into a large run beside the new chicken house. Just sitting on the bare ground, not pecking or scampering about, so obviously depressed them that we decided to let them run as they wished.

And though the coyotes eventually eliminated the chickens, the chickens that ran were the first to be caught. It took the coyotes some months to weave past the dogs and make a grab, and still they never got Big Red. She was different from the rest. Having survived longer than all the others, having broken all the rules for survival, neither fleeing nor fighting but remaining in the stillness, she outlived them all and died quietly in her nest, her glottis vibrating to Mozart.

* * *

Birds—on the ledge, in the sanctuary marsh, or scratching about the big coop—have long been one of my most precious intercessors with the shadow that turns life to stone. Birds are the only creatures that can cross the three natural elements.

They can walk on the earth, fly into the blue air and dream, and they can inhabit almost every realm, including water, as cormorants, loons, and pelicans plunge to fly beneath the waves.

We are born seeking wholeness. Birds can remind us of our original song, and of our acrobatic nature, and show us a beauty painted by the same brush as tropical flowers.

19. W H I T E   C L O U D S /
B L U E   S K Y

 **A**FTER THE FIRST SNOW, I go out searching for the music written in the crystal blanket. Snow allows the invisible to be seen. What has unfolded under a moonless sky is exposed by dawn.

After the last storm, sitting on a high outcropping, I look down to see the winding, intersecting trails of mice hemming the fresh snow. A fugue. The long foot of a jack rabbit indifferently criss-crossing the evidence of the hyperactive mouse's morning dash. It's as if a kettle drum punctuates the drifts. And near the bottom of the hill, a bloodspot at the foot of the earthen dam. Coyote tracks beside the opening of the rabbit's warren. There's Wagner in the wings.

In the afternoon, new tracks head up on the mesa. The wild burro we heard last week has passed through once again. I follow her unshod hoof prints—wild runes left by her midnight passing—until they disappear into a sudden rockface, where the snow has fallen away in the Zia sun.

I find near the top of the seven-hundred-foot incline the continuation of the tracks of this burro, lost from the herd, navigating by the stars. Down the ten-thousand-year-old deer trail, beneath the snow, are stone points and potsherds of pottery painted before the Conquistadors' deluge of European arrogance and brutal religion; afterward, the native peoples stopped painting their pots. These painted fragments mark the passing of whole continents of ourselves, mark all the forgetting it has taken for us to be left so violent and lost. Crossing the donkey's path, I notice the broad spoor of a mountain lion following its nose. A solitary elk watches through a pagoda juniper.

Joining the procession just behind the mountain lion, following its tracks one by one through the snow, each animal species' tracks are deeper than the last one's, almost graphing evolution and the food chain. This slow unfolding has an almost hypnotic effect. The pace slows, breath after breath, step after step, through the deep snow. The wind, a distant flute, raises a shimmering veil of snow, *tablas* on the inner ear.

Half blind from looking so long into the glistening snow, my mind stops using words to think. And for a few moments I see in images how an animal thinks. Animals don't hear music, animals *are* music. When we observe them closely, as Rodin reminded Rilke, it refines our seeing. Rodin said, "Go to the zoo and learn how to see!" So were born Rilke's poems "The Panther" and "The Swan." To see clearly is to open the Eye of Beauty, to hear with the inner ear, sitting quietly in the cave behind the tympanum, feeling as much as hearing the sounds unheard by most that fill the dark green paths of the animal world.

My breath becomes coordinated with paw print. Each breath is drawn in across the pure unruffled snow, then drops exhaled into the bottom of a fresh and perfect cougar print. My mind floats on the intersection of the lion's breath and mine as remnants of last night's dreams begin to surface.

One after another, my submerged dreams arise, then fade away, melting at their edges like the paw prints I'm following into the sun. There is a song to be found in the hard breath of climbing, a rhythm in the blood that remembers. No one is born in a house, that comes later.

And the puma leaps up the rockslide to the top of the *cerro* and becomes sky.

Standing in the midst of the glistening snowfield, I feel weeks of long forgotten dreams come flooding through. Some have sprung from a vagrant thought, or a milliwatt of fancy. Others have barely broken the surface and sink back down, waiting to get born, and there are those that were born against their will. And lovely dreams, stacked like prayer cloths, waiting to comfort devotees, ascending and descending from the storehouse of dreams, reveal the astounding contents of the heart.

I am dissolving out of my tracks, left too in the snow, laughing at nature's absurd perfection, shaking my head at human cruelty. We are here, present to the terrible/wonderful unfolding of creation and destruction, in the push and pull of gravity, in the concatenation of the stars.

The lion's steamy breath and the thin whistle of the frigid mouse are brought home to be entrusted to a poem, that place which is the altar of the heart, where precious memories reside in honor and gratitude. And when the heart and mind are in harmony, the flowers of humility can be offered on the *puja*.

20. BLUE SKY/ WHITE SNOW

the warmth in the breath, the patience in our marrow

IN THE SUN-SPATTERED, dappled forest, one can see the Earth breathing, and the spirit is not so easily denied. In such an authentic atmosphere, the monks are colorless and the tigers are allowed to keep their skin. All water is holy water. Seeing clearly, we find an invitation to liberation inside the clean-cut elk tracks and the dewy cobwebs at the bottoms of the coyote paw prints.

Some years ago, sitting quietly in the forest in the course of cultivating the "warmth and patience breath"—breathing in warmth and gradually exhaling on the outbreath—I came to believe that patience was the answer to all the world's problems. I breathed in the light of mercy, forgiveness, and the profound warmth the heart offers, then I exhaled, releasing ever so slowly and patiently on the outbreath, the holding, the forgetfulness, the mercilessness, the shadows. It seemed so startlingly simple that we shouldn't wait, anxiously or even aggressively, for God or the song, for liberation, for peace; but instead, we should rest in patience, where all things, including the mind in its wanderings, have room to grow and evolve. We need the patience of the cat and the tick and the old Zen master.

And I came to believe that humility was the most exquisite form of patience. That the "nature of mind" is "the mind of nature."

Also, that in the wisdom of the spoor can be found the hunter and hunted, the aging and the newly born—that impermanence and radiance rule the day. And patience leads to moments of that humility, absorbing the many into the one.

The samurai learns patience from the perfect arc of the long sword. He sits with the impeccable humility of a tick perched fifteen years at the tip of a twig or a large, yellow-spotted salamander hidden years in the dry pond bottom, no longer waiting for spring runoff or summer monsoons. The tick and the salamander are not waiting; they are instead absorbed in timelessness of patience—a patience that is at one with humility. It is here that humility and patience converge to form steadfastness without which we can go no further. We are like lotus seeds, which can germinate after lying for three thousand years on the pyramid floor. After having heard, from so unlikely a source as their own cells, that "being is enough" they let the blossom come forth from that last cell. They know from eons before language attempted to stop time that the timeless was the only hope we have, that the simple boundlessness behind it all was just enough. And the light by which it is seen, or better yet, that which experiences light, is more than enough. Exists long before "enough" and "not enough."

* * *

Standing at the foot of a two-hundred-year-old ponderosa towering above us, I bow. Each successive bow takes me deeper, closer.

At first I bow to the greatness of the tree, but by the time the next bow slowly evolves, I find I am bowing to the forest in which the tree and I both stand, and next bow is to all the beings in this forest which stretches for hundreds of miles well up into Colorado. And then, seeing a bit more, I bow to that quality that melds us all into that which we label "nature." The Ocean of Being is distributed out through nature's nerve currents as the life force pulsing at the heart of the ponderosa and in the heart of that which bows before it. We share the body of the planet, which floats like a whale in the forest, calling from ocean to ocean from here in the midst of all forests, all oceans resonating with the yearning, the longings of the soul-fire which lights the way of all sentient beings, all that dream or are about to dream, all that hope or have forgotten hope, all those who look and find all that they see "loveable." Of course, one might hear the above and feel that only a saint might see all things "as lovable," and that may be true, but one does not have to be a saint to make the seeing of beauty in such a remarkable manner their kind intention. And the bowing completes itself in the same silence in which it began, except for the coupling of the stars.

* * *

Beneath a great cottonwood by the stream, the only Bo Tree available, I find that awareness slowly turns to take itself as the object of awareness. Taking awareness as an object of awareness is like shining a spotlight into a mirror. Where all the objects of our present dreaminess and past confusion reflected our every move, only light suffuses.

But this light does not burn our eyes because there is intuitive trust in its nature, nothing need be clung to or condemned. The gatekeeper becomes a dance instructor. And the music, once so slow to arise, so fragmented, becomes trust in the process of awakening as the themes of gratitude and patience wind through our song, soft as the air within the nostrils when the breath settles and the heart becomes our new home. And at the gate, when asked the password, the aspirant can hardly hold himself or herself back. In a breath shared with all there is, we whisper, "Mercy and awareness." There is nothing realer than the clear light.

* * *

Sometimes, lost in an energetic stream of thought (emotion-fear-anger-doubt), walking a familiar path through the piñons and lupine, I once again remember. And I stand still, following consciousness to its component awareness, letting the thoughts roll on while I focus on the awareness by which the thoughts were perceived: awareness of awareness itself. And the edgeless ease, not only of my mindfulness of the objects of awareness, but of my direct experience of awareness itself, of bare attention, becomes the foreground of consciousness. The karma of thoughts falls away. The momentum of our identification with those thoughts, cultivated in previous moments of attachment, dissolves. As the thoughts themselves vanish from the luminous screen of consciousness, a little shudder moves like a wave through the body, and the energy propelling the line of thinking is released. What energy is in thought!

* * *

Things are quiet here. Spring begins to overflow into the valley and crawls up the side of the mountain. The buzzards and the hummingbirds have noticed, returning about an hour apart. The seasonal stream is trickling. Coyotes run the ridge with new cubs. And something greater than us all calls to us to make peace in the torn world, to learn to love even when we are in pain, even when we are frightened, to consider the well-being of others as we might that of our own children, and the prayer becomes *May All Beings Be Free From Suffering, May All Beings Be At Peace.*

21. MAD RAVEN TEACHINGS

 WHAT DO YOU DO if the resident ravens raise a full-grown fledgling child with some sort of brain anomaly that causes it to caw loudly about every three seconds, twenty times a minute, for weeks, sometimes quite near the house for hours, often outside our bedroom window at 5:30 a.m.?

One can feel the gut tighten when the mind notices the long repetition beginning once again. Then the mindfulness softens from caw to caw.

In the course of reflecting on possible solutions, I recalled the experiment so many years ago in Japan when, with the most sophisticated electroencephalograms, scientists measured brain reactions to long-repeated stimuli. The recurring ringing of a bell was noticed in the ordinary mind to slowly diminish in reaction as habituation to the stimuli occurred within a very few minutes. They hardly noticed it after a while. But when advanced students of Zen, and Zen masters, even more so Zen, were so measured it was noticed that each time the bell was rung, for no matter how many times, the same spiking of mindful response could be detected. They did not habituate, did not take bells or life for granted, and were completely present for each succeeding moment.

Could we use the raven's caw to bring us closer to the moment instead of following the ordinary aversion to uncontrollable—even unpleasant—repetition?

Often when quiet and present, we could receive the sound with no resistance and even experience a considerable concern for the raven's wellbeing. But often, when we are focused elsewhere, we find the sound an unwelcome intrusion. Yet what at first we resisted through fear and aversion we have gradually surrendered into with mercy and awareness.

Even now I hear our poor, brain-damaged ward down the valley, heading this way.

A few months ago, when we first heard the raven's long cawing, we thought that the bird would probably die soon from the birth defect that caused its unusual behavior.

And here it comes now, calling out in its own way "Karuna, Karuna" (compassion compassion), the way Aldous Huxley's myna birds made their statements and demands on his idealized island, in his last novel, the utopian *Island*. Settling on a nearby branch, our raven echoes those long-lost birds. Like

Huxley's myna, which shouted "Attention, attention," our raven calls out: "Here and now, boys! Here and now!"

The raven reminds us to soften, as well as that some questions, particularly those that deal directly with life, have no answer—that sometimes even love can't readily find a way.

Never was the need for surrender clearer or the fact that to honor the Buddha is to wash the feet of all sentient beings than it is in the presence of this poor raven.

* * *

The Tao of things never ceases to amaze me. Soon after writing the above, after nearly three months of experiencing the full range of emotion, from frustrated reaction to heartfelt response, our obsessive-compulsive young raven disappeared from the valley.

He was an excellent teacher.

22. HALF-A-CAT TEACHINGS

SOMEWHERE ALONG THE WAY, I was entrusted with a half-paralyzed cat. I used to bring her with me to the Unity Press office in a shoebox. Lying off to one side on my desk, she could be turned and fed as need be.

It may have been Joseph Goldstein, while working on his book, who first called her "Shoebox."

The cat's paralysis, the veterinarian said, made her "half a cat, a brain-oriented genetic failure" whose effects would progress up her body from her dragging back legs until she was completely unable to move and eventually unable to breathe. He reached out as if to take "this problem" off our hands. We replaced young Shoebox in her palanquin and off we went.

Three weeks, a hundred doses of a slowly swallowed concoction of warm olive oil with a smidgen of garlic, and many long massages later, the paralysis halted just before it hit her front legs. Gradually, it began to reverse itself. Then, about six weeks later, when she seemed to be sicker and was brought to me for some sort of animal last rites, she began doing the two-step on my meditation pillow.

But there was a moment when she was on her way back to health when, on what appeared to be a very bad day for her, she seemed to be losing strength very rapidly as the paralysis advanced back up her body. Meditating near her, I heard her dragging her back legs as she pulled toward me. So I lay with my back flat on the floor and put her on my chest. Thinking she might just die there, I let her just ride on the slow breath of meditation. About ten minutes into this process, she made a rasping breath and, it seemed, stopped breathing.

So I, half in faith and half immersed in some episode of Mystery Theater—the real illusion of birth-and-death—breathed my "breath-energy," heart-to-heart, back into her limp body. Perhaps, I thought, she had not died, or maybe she'd had a little kitty near-death experience and discovered that her body, like ours, was rented and not owned. But, with a shudder, she began once again to breathe. Opening her eyes close to mine, she burped, and I thought I smelled a little garlic.

Some months later, at 3:00 a.m., she jumped onto my bed, turned her rear-end to the side of my face and pushed her first baby into my ear.

23. SKUNK SATYGRAHA

 NE MORNING, about fifteen years ago, while living in our world of wildings in the forests of Northern New Mexico, a few days after nestling-in a few dozen chicks, I entered the coop to find a dozen of the chicks dead with their heads bitten off. Skunks!

We recognized our responsibility to chickens as well as the skunks, in whose territory we had plopped a tantalizing chicken coop, so rather than harming the skunks, we began improving the fencing under which they had apparently entered. We dug all day along the fence line and buried it well into the ground. Nothing short of a badger was going to dig its way through that enclosure.

But the next morning, there were more headless chicks.

We presumed the skunk had this time gone *over* rather than *under* the fence. It had seemingly climbed the chicken wire! We worked for most of the next day, clumsily stretching sagging chicken wire across the top of the pen. When the job was completed, we "knew" the few chicks remaining were at last going to be safe.

But next morning proved that we were wrong. Somehow the predator was still getting in.

We had exhausted all our nonlethal options, but, before taking more drastic measures, I decided to sit out one night in the well-fenced chicken yard in hopes of discovering their means of entrance.

After sitting outside in the cold for a few hours, I noticed that ego-glorifying, self-righteous sense of wounded innocence slipping in. Self-interest-above-all-else was accumulating. My anger was arising, and I was feeling increasing animosity for this remarkably resourceful though deadly invasive creature. *It was me against him.* I considered what sort of buckshot to use. I was slipping into a hunter identity. Catching my body hunching over, contracting like my mind, I spread wide my arms and arched my back to relieve the pressure. As my head tilted back, I looked up.

The enormous Southwestern sky was wild with fiery asteroids. It was the Perseid Meteor Shower. A half-dozen streaks of light at a time stretched across the sky. Never had I seen such a full display. One after another and then five at a time then crosswise another and another.

And, wanting to rest my neck, I looked back down. And there, not ten feet in front of me, was the skunk. He had slipped through what seemed far too slight an aperture between the corner post and the fence.

He was as beautiful as anything in creation. For a long moment, bathed together in a surreal star shower we looked deeply into each other's eyes. And beneath a singing sky, we simultaneously bowed and retreated.

I returned with hammer and nails to secure the corner fencing. The skunk went home and the sky kept on singing.

24. BATS

W HEN I WAS A CHILD, there was in common parlance the expression that someone might have "bats in their belfry," which meant they were a little "off their rocker." Ah, the colored streamers of language! Of course, having bats in your bell tower would cause a bit of a ruckus at the top of the skull. Except one should note that it is not the bats, which compose twenty percent of all mammals, that are stressed by being around humans; it is the violently more-than-animal territorialism of humans that wants bats away.

And, too, it need be recognized that most animals have a "stress radius" of a few feet or yards where humans will kill even those who are continents away because they say the "other" is trampling our interests! The Greeks called strangers "barbarians." Humans are a savage lot, though capable of grace.

When I was stewarding the sanctuary, a research scientist came to visit, seeking knowledge of any sightings we had had of the changes in some of the Mexican bats, as some individuals had begun switching from being insectivorous/carnivorous (blood suckers) to feeding from flowers (nectar sippers). As the collapse of the pollinating bee populations continues, already one-third in decline as I write, it may be these flower-kissing nectar eaters that will save crops, and thus the world—Apostate Dracula taking the Bach Flower cure for the benefit of us all. The research scientist had with her some bats to show me what remarkable creatures they were. I was particularly attracted to a "hog-nosed," actually kind of shovel-nosed beauty who had big black eyes like our favorite often-bewildered soft gray wood rat. She opened my heart cave to bats. I have always found them a most welcome and even friendly visitor.

When we lived near the base of the Rocky Mountains near Durango, Colorado, we had an old clapboard house which, in a wall beside the back deck, had a broken board. The area split off from the wide board was a few inches across. Inside the facing board, between the outer walls and inner walls, lived a bat colony. When we at first discovered them streaming out of the side of our house one sunset, we were a bit dismayed. "They will kill you in your sleep," a few people who had never lived outside a city warned us. "You'll get AIDS," their fear insisted. All, of course the sort of nonsense and exaggeration that ignorance anchored in fear depends on for its longevity.

We were somewhat concerned about rabies (this one not so fanciful), but since the county health officer had recently announced there was no rabies in the local animal populations at present, we felt no particular fear, but rather a sense of privilege to stand three feet back from the entrance to their lair and let them come streaming out past us. Though we stood only a few feet directly in front of their outpouring, never did one ever touch us. We stood in ecstasy in the ordaining flood of wings and high-pitched sonar squeals that plumed out into the rutting elk's bugling at dusk.

Now, some years later, some miles down the same mountain range, we note with delight that we have had a solitary bat that dips and flips about us for the last few summers.

Part 6

THE CELESTIAL HORDE

25. BEAR WALK

N OT BEING INITIATEd into the wide-spread Native American Bear Clan, I do not know what comprises a tradition-al Bear Walk, and can only relate what the "bear in me" experiences when it goes for a mindful trek into the Eye of Beauty.

In dreamtime, the solitary red bear wanders into clearings in the mind, paws the flesh of the earth, rolls logs for morsels, and pumps those iron back legs up the mountain into the sky.

Walking and singing, feeling the breath rising and falling near the heart releases the mind. Placing one foot before anoth-er on the sacred earth, like one word of the song after another, one breath after another, we feel the body lean and sway as it finds its own gait, following the innate rhythms of the natural mind in the natural body. Not *thinking* the walk but letting go of ideas about walking, *letting the bear walk*. Like letting go of con-trol of the breath to let the breath breathe itself, we let the body free itself to walk on its own without support of the propped-up mind—walking in a sacred manner, as the native peoples say.

The first mindful steps are slow and gradual as we invite the spirit bear (like Manjushri, the Tibetan celestial whose swift sword cuts through the morass, clearing the overgrown trail to clear the path), to soften her great belly, to stand and stretch her arms, to extend her fingers curled like claws, to growl and growl louder to call the forests to peace, waving aside the hindrances that plague the bear in us, the anger and fear of strangers, the blood lust (the panda has taken the bear spirit to heart and no longer kills to survive, is no longer a carnivore but a bemused browser of bamboo forests) and the sometimes agonizing longing to know our Great Nature without owning the gods or forgetting compassion.

Soon the willingness to feel the "bear energy" (incidentally, in meditation, we are often told to exercise "bare attention" when observing man and nature) and use it to let go—to soften rather than harden and hold on for dear life to that which causes us suffering—gentles the ferocious ego. We find at first the mind does all the walking, then, gradually, the body takes over a step at a time and soon we find it is the heart we are walking through. It becomes like the musical staff on which the notes are written. Thoughts flow through the great heart of the sprit bear walking beside us; we sense an unexpected, inexplicable happiness, the joy of rolling in the meadow, of scratching our back against a rough pine, of clearing the path to the entrance to the heart.

Step by step, we refresh the body. Gradually, the mind begins to note the sensations in each step, feeling the muscles lift the foot, then swing it forward, then place it back on the ground. We note the moment when both feet touch the Earth before the next foot rises to the challenge and attend to the moment-to-moment sensations that accompany each step; it is as though we are learning to walk all over again. We imagine what it must have been like to take our first steps as an infant or a cub. A sense of accomplishment rarely rivaled arises in our newborn body and mind, in our original heart.

We walk through the field of sensation noting how our awareness becomes more precise. Watching the beginning, middle, and end of each step, perhaps in the same manner we notice the beginning, middle, and end of each thought before it blends into the next. And as our focus sharpens, we may, for an instant, see the spaciousness of awareness which buoys equally our joy and sorrow.

Resting in the dappled shadow of an ample tree, we sit quietly, reflecting on how hardened our belly has become, fruitlessly trying to protect itself from pain. And honoring the pain-ridden abdominal muscles holding the grief long-stored in our belly, we send the bear of mercy to bring loving kindness into it.

It takes a while to get out of our own way and become quiet as a bear silently surveying its surroundings. Slowly, what was invisible becomes visible. An ant purposefully scouting for the tribe. A bee testing pollen. A cloud that reminds us of something. Gradually, what was unheard attracts the inner ear. Bird songs vary. The wind sings differently from tree to tree. We settle through levels and levels of quiet. We breathe in warmth and mercy, slowly, patiently, through those great bear nostrils, breathing out the holding, the forgetfulness, the mercilessness, which shadows us.

In fortunate moments, the patience of the bear becomes startlingly simple. There is no waiting for God or liberation. Resting in patience, everything has room to be as it is. Nature and mind are within each other as "the nature of mind."

Surrendering our impatience, we find something too beautiful for words. Blue skies and white clouds.

Sometimes the spirit bear (a state of mind of profound compassion and unbreakable commitment to the wellbeing of others) ambles next to a grieving child or sits by a dying deer with a broken back and tries to soothe its fear. Sometimes it works, but sometimes the pain is even bigger than the bear and she can do nothing but weep in helplessness.

I remember once walking for a long time through the vacuum created by the death of a dear friend. I never needed the bear of mercy and awareness more. At first, weeping and a strong desire to turn around slowed my steps. Walking like a bear through the wall of resistance, I continued talking to my dear friend in my heart.

Eventually, the loneliness, the unfinished business, the remorse caused me to sit trembling by the path as long-forgotten memories came flooding into the astounding capacity of my heart. And I delighted that so great a chasm of loss could coincide with a feeling of love so great it soothed the broken world.

Taking one step after another, though at times we may fear we will become lost, we eventually find our way home.

26. THE BANDITS AND THE BLOWFISH

IN THE JEEP WE RENTED from the hotel in Puerto Vallarta, we followed the curve of the belly of Banderas Bay, with the green sea reaching toward and retreating from the shore along the way, like a giant green sea turtle attempting to pull itself onto the rising beach—the turtle so hypnotized by the rhythm of the waves, that it lolls in the surf, dreaming it is a curved bubble at the tip of a great wave.

The sea turtle recalled its lovely strength in early myths, in which it created the world and bore it on its back, the distant edge of its great carapace one of the ten thousand tectonic plates of the universe on which the planets and stars float, and after which many gods were named.

Ondrea and I sat in the Jeep on a deserted beach at the end of a labyrinth of sandy roads penetrated by the near-equatorial sun on the fertile body of what earlier inhabitants of the hemisphere called Earth Mother Tortoise, Turtle Island, Universe-Without-End. We, too, floated in the turtle sea, in the pools behind the retina, in our salty remnants of the sea from which we were created. We dreamed of creation and the warm winds which opened the womb of the Earth and brought forth evolution.

Walking the isolated beach, we picked up cowry and clam shells, pieces of pearly abalone. The crush could be felt in the shards, the tentacles pulling in, the beak descending, a cloud of ink obscuring the blameless cruelty that survival often requires—the necessary cruelty we are shy to admit, but if the robin didn't eat the worm, the world would come to an end in about a week.

I looked for the waxy lumps of ambergris, the sperm whale's legend, laid by the tide in a nest of scrimshaw in the hard sand at the edge, passing for the second time a dead blowfish, the kind you might find hollow and dried stacked in a pile in a souvenir shop, the sort people occasionally turn into a small lamp. The blowfish is the fish served as a sushi to the brave of heart and weary of gut in Japan. It is known as the *fugu*, and if it is improperly prepared to be eaten, its nerve toxin can kill. It is the Russian roulette of fish consumption.

One might view the blowfish as something of a demon. Stabbing and poisoning its quarry, it rises from the depths to swell, great and ominous, before those creatures that were once its size.

That day on the beach, as we passed the blowfish, Ondrea felt that perhaps even though there was no movement in the creature, it might well still be alive, so she most carefully and with great respect picked up the seemingly dead fish and placed it back into the sea. Before the blowfish was even completely covered by the water, it shook off death and sped off at a remarkable rate. "It made a quick salutary circle and sprinted away home," Ondrea said. It was a remarkable transformation, not unlike the stories related of near-death experiences, where one might go from laboriously releasing the last breath to turning into something akin to light, fast as thought, sprinting toward the vast beyond. I have heard it said that death makes us a fish out of water. I suspect it may be just the opposite—a return to the Great Sea.

Quite involved in the process of releasing the blowfish, we were a bit surprised when we looked up and saw that four local men were approaching us, coming too close too fast. My poor yet sometimes serviceable Spanish made some sort of greeting and I watched their eyes as they looked us over, particularly Ondrea. They asked us were we were from but before we could really answer, one of them said, "You know Spanish men are muy amoroso." I felt my belly tighten further, thinking we might well be in for a very bad time. And just then over the crest of a low dune came three peasant-bloused, flower-skirted young women, who called to the men by name, causing them to step back quickly from what might have appeared to be exactly what it was. The women flowed down the slope of the dune as if surfing, cutting through the surf of the sand like the blowfish had cut through the surface current that drew it deeper. They were like the *gopis*, the shepherdesses that so loved Krishna, that many believe were under his guidance and protection but were in fact his saviors, his ground, and his lamp, though even the gods are sometimes reticent to admit their needs or weaknesses.

It has long been rumored that to free a demon can bring protection and guardianship. Demons can teach us how to love by watching how unloving we can be. Taking the thorn from the paw of a wild beast, according to folktales, can bring about both friendship and the promise of safety.

Indeed, that is the case in the story about the great Tibetan Buddhist hermit Milarepa who freed the demons of their egotistical attachment to the fruits of their labors. He provided them with one of the great evolutions, it is said in the Bhagavad Gita, which is the resolution of karmas, the basis of karma yoga; indeed, it is the very definition of renunciation. To save a demon is to depopulate the hell realms of the mind, to take another step forward.

Ram, a legendary Hindu divinity, freed the demon king Ravana in the classic Ramayana. Ravana had done just about everything he could, including stealing Ram's beloved Sita to get Ram's attention, to force a confrontation between them. It resulted in a long, ferocious battle employing supernatural weapons and considerable magical powers. And at last the demon Ravana was slain. But the next day, in a letter designed to be delivered after his death, the demon revealed to Ram that his actual intention was born of his admiration for Ram, that all his fierce troublemaking was just to fight to the death with Ram and "to be killed by God."

On that day, Ondrea freed the spiny spirit of the blowfish and the consorts of Krishna flowed down from the sky, surfing the dunes, to protect us and sweep away the obstacles to love.

27. DRAGONS

THE DRAGON IS REJECTED by only a few cultures for being demon-like. Those cultures are the naturally earthbound faiths like Christianity, which rejects the dragon because it is part reptile, and therefore was cursed in Eden.

But the dragon has incorporated the wisdom of one whose belly touches the earth while lifting off, pushing outward into space. And the dragon is also supposed to breathe fire while living in its secret lake. It is fire and water, earth and sky—all the elements of balance, all we need to progress further.

The dragon wants the world to know he did not offer the apple in the Garden of Eden. He only said, "There is no death." He only said, "The world is a dream." He only said, "The world needs to become real in your heart for the healing to begin." He only said, "Love each other as you might yourself." He only said, "If you can forgive yourself, you can forgive anyone." He only said, "Take all the mortis and

Christ-is-not-allowed-down-from-the-cross and toss them into the ocean." He only said, "There is a temple and a wailing wall waiting in the heart." He only said, "Be present and make kindness your only religion."

And ever after the Dragon has been hunted, by some as the spawn of the obstructive states of mind, when in truth, the very etymology of the word *dragon* means "to see clearly." Clarity has long been the bane of blind faiths that do not so much love the object of their adoration as attempt to own it. The Dragon drops from the rafters like Manjushri with his sword extended to cut away our fears and fetters, to liberate us, with that slight nausea that often precedes great insight, with the stomach softening to let loose, to release, the insistence on a particular reality, as the aperture widens until what reality means changes.

In the bardo, in the vastness between planes of reality, the Interstitial Dragon appears quite at home. She is the space between thoughts, the "seeing beyond" for which she is so appreciated even by those who don't know or believe she exists. In the old terms, she could almost be lexigraphed into hardly existing at all. She says it is as true to say she exists as it is to say she doesn't, she would not quarrel with either. Being as much the vastness between the seeming solidity of thoughts as she is the swirling *maya* of thought itself, she does not take sides, but suggests mercy where friction might occur. When stopping somewhere, the cerebellum stumbles over "This is my—the only—reality," lessening the investigation of who indeed it is that reads this, writes this, likes or dislikes, opens or closes, loves truth or doesn't. Who sits in quiet and learns to breathe without fear, disturbing the breeding place and legendary homesite of the flying serpent that carries time like a pearl in its timeless ruby teeth? If it were not for timelessness, time could not exist.

Abstract and fanciful as all this may be, each of us is between decisions. Each of us is in the space, the bardo, between incarnations. Each choice can accentuate the reptilian survival-at-any-cost medulla oblongata base brain or the dream-filled, flight-bound frontal lobes.

The dragon is as real as you are. And the deeper you go, the less definable you become. Changing phylum would be the least of it.

28. HANUMAN AND GANESHA

THE CELESTIAL MONKEY HANUMAN

 THE TRANSCENDENT ANIMAL SPIRIT Hanuman is a remarkable personification of devotion and selfless service in the classic Hindu holy book, the Ramayana.

In the Ramayana, Hanuman, a great white ape, served Ram, a manifestation of God, without reserve. Indeed, Hanuman nearly defines devotional practice (bhakti yoga) when, to show how complete his absorption is in the sacred, he pulls open his chest to reveal the name of God, Ram, written on every bone in his body.

Hanuman, holding open his chest to display the heart of devotion, is one of the most popular sacred images in India. This bloody tearing-open to reveal our true nature may be reminiscent of the image of Jesus hanging from the cross. Though the images may seem quite different, their blood is the same.

It makes us ask, "How long will it take our Jesus to get our Antichrist down from the cross?" It's the sort of question that only a devoted ape would dare to ask. What will it take for us to remember? How long will we live, trembling at the foot of the cross, until we drop to our knees before the divine within?

Tiring of glory, it is said, Jesus had to let himself down. Following the curve of the hill his feet took a moment to reach the ground.

Mistaken for Buddha, mistaken for Krishna, mistaken for God, he got drunk like a Tang hermit, coming down from the mountain with a few poems tucked in his robe and the amazing light of Being leaking through, only allowed to play with the children. "Crazy old man!" And the earth felt so good to his scarred feet, mud between the toes more distinct than the fading heavens. "Nothing true but love," he said. No matter that the gods of war proclaim that you can count on fear more than love.

Standing like Arjuna in the Glorious Gita, or is it Arjuna himself out there, up to his knees in corpses and the sharp tools that create corpses? On the battlefield, the God of Love, the God of Peace, arms extended pierced by a torrent of arrows revealing the name of their beloved in every language, on every heart, on every bone, the ribcage like a cathedral, the altar of the heart still red with sacrifice and the cool blue of letting go like Hanuman in the Ramayana: Ram's name incised on every bone as is the longing of saints.

THE ELEPHANT-HEADED GOD GANESHA

 IN INDIA, one of the most popular household gods is Ganesha, the elephant-headed deity considered a master of intellect and wisdom. He is depicted as a big-bellied, yellow or red god with four arms and the head of a one-tusked elephant; he rides on or is attended to by a mouse.

Ganesha's elephant head symbolizes the supreme reality. His human body signifies maya or the confusions, even illusions, of the earthly existence of human beings. Ganesha's trunk represents the sound Om, on which the universe is strung, the tone innate in our cells, the password to the whole of us. In his upper right hand, Ganesha holds a divining rod which guides our evolutionary unfolding. The noose in Ganesha's left hand lassos our ancient hindrances. We enter alive in the moment. We sense the Presence in presence. In Ganesha's wake, only edgeless presence remains, nothing to obstruct lucidity or distract us from the ground of being.

Hanuman knew it well when he said to Ram, "When I do not know who I am, I serve You. But when I know who I am, I am You."

Ganesha broke off his trunk to write the Mahabrata. The string of prayer beads in his other hand suggests that the inquiry into existence should be continuous. The snake that runs round his waist represents energy in all forms.

And he is humble enough to ride the lowest of creatures, a mouse. (This, it turned out for me, was the mouse of faith on which I rode down the mountain.)

One day I was given a small brass Ganesha from India. I put it in a niche in the rock wall behind which my mother's ashes are buried. It has been there for years. Occasionally, when I visit that rock outcropping, I have found a large porcupine sitting near the small brass statue. He is very slow to move and will never go farther than the opening beneath a rock tumble a few yards away. I have at times sung on that ledge to the muffled grunts of the Guardian Porcupine, who sits like a Kara Shi Shi, a Japanese temple dog guarding the way, waiting for the two-legged being to move on.

29. DREAMTIME VISITORS

 I HEAR THE DRUMS; it is the dreaming time. Slowly, the lens closes. Sleep enters like a welcome guest. The table is already set as for Elijah or Shiva's tigers. This is the most remarkable set of dreams so far. I have dreamed of the Dalai Lama and most of my teachers, and I have been even initiated in dreams, taught and experienced unimaginable insight, the teachings opening into grace, the Dharma in Technicolor, but none have stayed with me like the animal dreams. Dreamtime comes as the iris opens wide

behind closed lids. (Iris is interestingly the Greek Goddess of the Rainbow, and a messenger of the gods. She is invoked in dreams. The REM fluttering is the beating of her wings.)

Dreamtime brings us back to life. In dreamtime, the sacred and the capacity to recognize the sacred are wed.

4:00 A.M. ONDREA, WAKING, SITS IN MEDITATION.

Buddha recommended meditation
in "the third watch of the night"
in that stillness, in that darkness
the light becomes most intense

at the dark window numberless faces
dissolve one into the wretched next
in crowds that push forward
for her blessing
and each gets what they came for
an open heart attracts the penitent
from other worlds.

In the first of my dreams, in a not-unusual home setting, a black panther casually crossed the room. I was surprised to find my admiration for his shimmering beauty rather than my fear predominating. It was like something out of a Rousseau painting—the dreamer and the lion.

The dream continued the next night, and the black panther was with two tawny mountain lions. There was a distinct feeling that they had been brought to further clear my perception of the accustomed fear of danger, the unknown, even death. The large cats emitted a warmth and even a friendliness. They came and laid beside me next to the stream. One big female and I listened together to the water flowing. We may have even entered each other's sensory field, she hearing as I might and I flicking my pointed ears, like hitting the refresh button on a computer, to "clear the air." I experienced how much more she heard of the chiming in the water than I did through my diminished sensory imagination. I think she felt a true sadness for me. Her SATs were a good deal higher than mine. And a sense really of family, of long familiarity and trust. It was a humming delight.

I awoke remembering a series of dreams I had once had, in which I awoke each morning for a week or more feeling as though I had received a great teaching. I even played with the idea for a while that I was getting teachings from what others have called the Ascended Masters. Whatever was happening in those moments of interbeing, I arose each morning with the feeling of having read a great spiritual work during dreamtime, but it, like all such "extended experience," is just to be directly absorbed (into a preverbal depth that knows it all but just can't express it and is relieved in waves of calm to feel its fur against another), not slowed by an attempt to understand or control. A happiness ensued that is our birthright. During that series of dreams, I awoke each day ecstatic.

In the next dream, the largest of the mountain lions was sitting beside Ondrea in the garden. The lion and Ondrea were talking, very friendly. And when Ondrea was concentrating on some row planting, the steel gray cat seemed to just enjoy surveilling the tree line nearby. He was purring, and in his amber eyes were black holes that led to panther paradise. I wondered, after this quiet little dream, if perhaps I was just dream-seeing what I was normally blind to. I have often thought that Ondrea is part of the sisterhood of earthen wisdom, but it would be unlikely that her familiar would be a small black pussycat; rather, it would be that enormous presence that sat so lovingly, so powerfully protective, beside her.

In a fragment of another dream, I was sitting on a slight hill in a wooded area, looking across a river at a metropolis. There was, I recall, a half dozen wolves that approached slowly and with their heads raised in an inquisitive manner. They looked me over like I was an exchange student from some exotic country. They were quite humorous in their play and chased their tails like puppies, howling and jumping, having big fun in the phylum.

But, looking back at the city, at the highway that ran along the river, I could see the head and neck of a giraffe running frightened in the traffic. First, the head and neck were transported by the unseen, running, terrified body a mile one way and then a mile in the other direction. This vision of a terrified wildling caught in the midst of heavy traffic, this helplessness pressing against the heart—plunging for death just as surely as Robinson Jeffers' eagle, dying in the impact, "struck/Peace like a white fawn in a dell of fire"—this loss of evolution.

The next dreams began in an empty open-air restaurant in the midst of the jungle. It reminded me of years ago in Mexico. The food is that kind of food one finds particularly at frond-roofed open shacks beside a road with a garden in back and today's meat hanging fresh-killed in the shed. In the dream, half-finished, I left the meal to look at something I sensed in the surrounding jungle. I knew my food would still be there when I returned. I followed a short path between dense foliage into a large clearing, where two very large tigers, perhaps six hundred pounds each, were standing about two hundred feet away. Slowly, they began to approach, but I can't really tell you many details as my belly started to harden and my mind produced fear. But I noticed that it wasn't the fight-or-flight kind of fear; it was more like the slight nausea that you feel before the Beloved reveals itself to you, the slight bottomlessness on the verge of impermanence. Lack of control was approaching on golden paws. And my heart somehow spontaneously opened to the expectation of love. The cats came forward as if to a brood mate. They wrapped themselves around my legs, they grazed me with tongues smooth as silk. (Dream tigers are usually the upgraded models, whose perfectly functional abrasive tongues will no longer drag the flesh from the bone but rather will heal wounds and sorrow with an extra-worldly caress.) When I returned from the clearing to the restaurant, there on the table, where I had left it, was my plate of food, warm and still ready of be consumed.

In subsequent dreams, the tigers had a somewhat unusual coloring: a maroon stripe between the usual yellow, black, and white markings. It blended so perfectly, but these cats were yet larger and the usual fear would arise by itself upon my seeing them and then quickly disappear when they approached. One of them came right up to me and, looking into my eyes, opened its mouth. I knew what was to be done and it seemed as necessary as learning to read. And I laid my head inside his cavernous jaws onto his pink pillow of a tongue. And I am not sure of what happened next, perhaps my mind stopped in between thoughts, went deeper than thought, so naturally there is no recollection, but I had a feeling of being loved and of loving as I have seldom known.

And between this dream and those that followed, in which I always ended up putting my head in the tiger's mouth, I recognized the maroon stripe. It was Tibetan maroon. It was the color of His Holiness the Dalai Lama's robes. We had had a few dances and he had stolen my heart. It was the Dalai Lama telling me, as Mirabai did centuries earlier, that if I wanted to be free of obstructive tendencies and conditioning to "cut off my head and sit on it"—that it takes that level of perseverance and self-acceptance to make it through what Buddha called the hindrances harder to overcome than a thousand-thousand foes, to become invisible except to those who can truly see.

To put your head in the tiger's mouth is to follow the "high path with no railing."

30. RIDING THE MINOTAUR ACROSS THE STELLAR MAZE

 WE COME AS CHILDREN, with nursery rhymes of God, and birds singing at our bedroom window. We come as children, through years of confusing grace, to find that what we are looking for is looking back at us, and our suffering brings us closer.

Ramakrishna tapped Vivekananda with his toe and spun him through solar systems Jung feared and longed for, and opened to me the first wisdom door I walked through. Now, again, he calls to me all these years later, still living in that book, opening a passageway to the actual.

We come naked at last to the truth, dismayed until the last moment before, then expectant of the inborn gift breaking the horizon. Oh, full moon. Oh, the surging upward. Oh, the shining within everything. Oh, the humility and gratitude.

We come as children, fumbling with our lives, tripping and bruising; for a moment, balancing on both feet to find our way through the labyrinth into our inmost dwelling.

From the center, we follow the curving upward into space and the settling downward as well, riding the Minotaur* across the stellar maze. The oxen are fed and stabled with the deer. The singing in the temples bridges the mind. The prayer is everywhere the same.

* * *

Ondrea dreams of such *disordinary* creatures from other worlds who follow disheartened pilgrims seeking blessings into her dreams.

The Minotaur is installed in the labyrinth by shame. It is a classical representation of one of the great hindrances to "our inmost dwelling" to which ancient peoples made human sacrifices, but to which today we sacrifice ourselves.

---

* The Minotaur is a crossover teacher from the celestial herd—part human, part animal, said therefore to be *the offspring of the unholy, a misalliance between man and nature*—fiercer than the star-born Centaur and a good deal less vain.

The Minotaur patrols the labyrinth, the well-worn paths between the mind and the heart, between forgetfulness and the soul. We navigate past the nymphs of forgetfulness and track the warm beast, drawn by the siren-call at the center and our long preparation for clarity.

To ride the Minotaur, having come and gone from the rodeo of thinking, some ethereal aspect of ourselves may surface long enough to help us decipher the Zen pictography of the Ten Oxherding Pictures. I am forced on my knees before it, no short, bloodstained sword sequestered behind my cape.

And the bull settles to his knees as well and bids me to hoist myself upon his broad back. He is no longer trying to kill or corral the Manjushri beast, the cutter of fetters, not even to herd him. My solar plexus is loosened, stars escape, and the bull rises through Taurus; now, we are one, following the arc toward morning and awakening.

From this perspective, there are no inner or outer, no endings or beginnings, no momentary diamond, no constellations or thoughts blocked. The goal is an obstacle, nothing absent. Capable of revealing the hard-won source, the watcher and the watched are simple eternities gathering myths, archetypal truths, with the proviso that they are not true.

But what are we to do when we can be God but can never know God? When we cannot put our finger on it anywhere, we look in or out of ourselves. But we sense its presence—the hot breath of God on the back of our neck, the beast turned accomplice in the search.

* * *

THE BESTIA AMOUR

One of the animals that may visit us in our sleep is the Bestia Amour, the Love Beast that devours all that is not at least at times loved. It eats our karma and leaves us with new furniture. There is a television commercial for a plastics company that demonstrates what the world would be without their product, and the viewer sees phones and surgical apparatuses and automobile interiors and the thousands of objects in which plastic is a major element, all melt away and disappear. The Love Beast is like that, but it is all which is unloved that disappears. As Dostoevsky noted, all that is unloved decomposes quickly.

And it doesn't just stop at what you would like to be rid of, but all that was not attended to in mind, body, or even spirit. A wasteland remains, but the ground is fertile. And the Bestia Amour helps sow seeds and drags its lovely tail to furrow the rich soil. And what grows in this blessing/dream is climbing stalks of loving kindness, and rows of flowering mercy. He is the drumming and the drummer, he is what love creates and romance can destroy, he is what compassion can sow and our self-centered trickery can obscure. Feeding ourselves with both hands, we have nothing left to offer. The Bestia's open maw is a flowing cornucopia of wisdom. The Bestia is the Interstitial Dragon, representing the next evolutionary step, the leap to a new species. Gary Snyder said that we are primitives of a distant civilization. The force for clarity, which is the wisdom element in love, drives the unfolding. In Darwinism, it is not new ways to survive that is the sole evolutionary momentum, but the wisdom that drives an innate wonderment, that maps migratory routes and love poems in all of us "four-footeds and uprights" for use when the time comes.

Does the Bestia Amour, free to leap unimagined chasms and present the possibility of another sense to our repertoire, become the Minotaur when his vision is imprisoned?

Part 7

END GAME

31. RETURNING TO THE CABIN, WITNESS

THIRTY YEARS LATER I revisited my old life, climbing the old mountain, following the path that leads more than thirty years back to the cabin. The trail seemed longer without Noah's small hand in mine, without Tara picking flowers as we gradually climbed.

But the vague evening deer and the shimmering morning lupine remembered. And the river we walked through when we left the world together remembered, too, when the forest grew from our shoes, and bobcats nestled in the milk case by the old sequoia.

I found my way without rain, back to my shadow waiting patiently for my return. Ghosts and demons had set a friendly table. There was nourishment for my journey-self, already waiting by the door, to get going further up the mountain, past the tree line, up where that final haiku might be found.

3 2 . A M A N R E A D S P O E T R Y T O A C A T I N A N E M P T Y W A R E H O U S E : A N I N V E N T O R Y O F L I F E

A KIND MAN SITS DOWN *to read to a lonely cat in an abandoned warehouse. He comes to visit every day or two to continue letting the cat know about the world outside, the world in its genes:*

Lightning mesmerizes the sky. It changes night to day. It calls out the stars. Gayatri.

The wind makes harps of the brittle grass.

The fat summer sun breaks over the purple rim of mountains. Valleys fill with gold. There are a thousand waking wrigglings: ebony staghorn beetles rise from prehistory, they shine like obsidian. The world of insects stretches and flutters, all the cold-blooded, scaly rainbow-gatherers, the refractors of the sun gods. Ahura Mazda.

The first shafts of light lift a golden eagle from her ledge. She looks down on the stirrings of rabbits and soft gray wood rats. Her two eaglet chicks, big as rabbits themselves, wait noisily for breakfast's return.

Birds, migrating up from Mexico and down from the Arctic, fill the high deserts with a hundred different flight patterns. Rising from agave fortresses in the high Sonoran desert grasslands, slaloming through Spanish bayonet and serrated yuccas, the explorers set forth. Rainbow, hedgehog, and prickly pear cactus bless the dry lands; cholla's spring magenta emboldens their religiosity. In the shadowy ravines, dominated by the shamanic jimson, are the quarter-sized hoof prints of the porcine god, Javelina, the wild in wildlife. Coyotes run the rim, seeking darting morsels but never the warrior pig who so loves the moon.

Bighorn sheep stand silhouetted against the red and purple shale of the mountainside. A black bear waddles across a cattailed marsh. He is lonely since the animal paths were turned to roads.

The turkey vulture is shiny black with its crop as red as the signature in a Sumi scroll. A circling red-tailed hawk stirs the stew. Beside the minnow-filled stream, under a squaw bush, a tiny ground dove shrugs night from its soft feathers, while mourning doves and white-winged doves coo their approval of the day. A conference of band-tailed pigeons breaks from the walnut trees and heads toward the buffet of the meadow. The ghost memories of the black-footed ferret still leave wet slides in the dew. The burrowing owl remembers.

33. THE CAT ROLLS OVER AND RESTS ITS HEAD ON THE READER'S OTHER SHOE

THE KIND MAN CONTINUES:

Gray fox, venerated in many fables, keeps her promise, leaping into the thick marsh, throwing stars into the air. In Zen, the gray fox is old masters and wily teachings. On the Northwestern coast of Canada, the whale was totem teachings. And the seal. And large black birds with blessing yellow eyes. And all the other gods that convened to potlatch with the human spirit, to bring the mind that separates into the heart that unites, the sacred hoop, the innate teacher of the sacred manner.

And then the crows and ravens swoop from the desert floor up the side of the mountains, up to the tree line, and dive with Clark's Nutcracker into the pinion forests, scattering husks like rose petals at a wedding.

Crows are spirit messengers. They are the dark angels that marked the rebirth far from Lhasa. Our pueblo neighbors tell tribal legends, bone-stories, of the crow and its greater cousin Raven. Crows gossip a lot and only talk of earthly matters. Their wings are shiny, but not quite broad enough for the heavens. But they say Raven sits at His table, acrobating black prayer flags.

Animals, too, sleep in the Mystery.

34. LA CIENEGA

THE SUN DRAPES from the hundred-year-old cottonwoods by the stream. It falls to the stream bank in dappled portions of gold over the green moss and the black stones, stippled with the silver dew. Such a wonderful place to sit quietly and breakfast on the wild asparagus that escaped decades ago from an upwind farm. A coatimundi, a South American cousin of the raccoon, chatters in an Emory oak, his two-foot-long tail whipping back and forth its limited salutation/warning a few feet up the incline that leads from O'Donnell Basin onto the pronghorn grasslands that follow, tight as a school of fish, the intuitive communal acrobatics, turns, and leaps of the group—that "gyre and gimble in the Wabe."

And, just on the other side of a row of quince and apple and pecan trees planted eighty years ago by the frontiersman Whitehill, who is buried under the front porch, is the treasure marsh, the only water for miles, the migration local for a hundred and twenty-five species of southern and northern birds meeting at the far end of their migratory route. The ground is soaked just beneath the surface, a "cienega" as it is called in these parts, indeed, the name of the Nature Conservancy reserve is the Canelo Hills Cienega. It's the boggy home for sedge and an abundance of buttercups, blue-eyed grass, rare primrose, violets, and a sea of wildflowers, all jewels. Dozens of nests and burrows convene life in sanctuary. And the rare orchid *Spiranthes graminea*, whose tiny white trumpets swirl toward the sun, is found again praising the sun for the first time in thirty years. Rushes, spicebush, and tulles are conspicuous in their "old boy" conspiracies.

The vermilion flycatcher sings to morning as he glides across the green eye of the cienega oasis, seeking a mate with his crimson acrobatics. His shadow brushes over a rabbit sitting huddled, its shoulders held like a cape up to the sides of his head, attempting invisibility in the shadow of a swooping prairie falcon. A cotton rat captured in the steel gray coils of a gopher snake shrieks its death haiku. *"Screeee. I cannot stop ending."*

Like the falcon, the cienega is an endangered species, a water relic of sad old glaciers weeping deep water tables as they retreated back up into the icecap. In the cattail's shadow, the lilting song sparrow and the self-conscious rail find their way following the song path of the red-winged blackbird who's yodeling atop a fat cattail, a heraldic squire of the marsh beneath a giant mulberry tree whose roots are carpeted with cress. In the song floats the bursting of cattails pouring cotton-winged seeds like floating syllables about to settle into a long epic poem or a one-word haiku: *"Swah!"* It says: *I am alive. I love, therefore I am.*

Birds brag about being so very alive. They have a song when the sun appears and one when it is dropping away, they call to lovers and enemies with song and their elocution is perfect. I have never heard a bird lie. Or a gray fox hanging half a rabbit in a bush for later consumption. Though many species tend to camouflage or even imitate another's fearsome appearance, as gopher snakes shaking their harmless tails to imitate the rattlesnake, they do not lie.

Beside the cienega is the eighty-year-old, two-and-a-half-foot-thick-walled adobe, whose northern wall had no windows but rifle slots to fend off the attacking Apache. It is home too for various species of mice come indoors for winter from the grassy fields. A large gray rock squirrel sits under the eves, a mountain king snake departs from the broken-walled end of the old house. Through the saguaro rafters can be seen the webs, eggs, and migrations of the insect people. An alligator lizard high on the wall is our best indoor insecticide. Though we are committed to the stewardship of the land, we are learning to be simple, not simpletons, thus discouraging the presence of a rare rock rattler and a black-tailed rattler, encouraging them to return to the community of dreaming dragons about to leap free from dreamless sleep, the Sonoran whip snake, the gopher snake, the ring-neck snake, and several designs of garter snake, all of whom we gently broom off the porch into the grasslands that swallow the house. A horned toad, orange and dusty, peers up from the corner of the porch, questioning his reptilian place, as a pygmy mouse scampers for protective shade away from Sir Rattler's diamond eyes.

The afternoon sun slides across the meadow and passes through the house, then climbs the oak grassland hillside that rises from behind the house to the enchanted mesa. The white star lily, the pink-flowered succulents, and the mandala-topped rainbow cactus hold the passing sun as long as they can. The nights can be cold. But this is daytime, the sun, the sweet marsh, the clear stream—they came all this way for it. From Mexico, the *caracara* traps the warm breeze between its glistening primaries, the gray hawk is up too, to feast at the sanctuary. The green kingfisher, a squawking relative of the common belted kingfisher, sings the old songs with the other South American repatriates, the trogon and the becard and the tropical kingbird—secret songs that tell of the hidden heart of Machu Picchu.

From the south come long-feathered colors and beaks able to reach through a thousand miles of jungle and mountain flourishings to pick a lion ant from a tiny divot in the soft sanctuary soil. And from the north, from the evergreen forests of Canada, the red crossbill and the evening grosbeak into the overlapping range. Escaping the snow-dense woodlands, too, are the goshawk, marsh, and rough-legged hawks. The yellow grosbeak, the five-striped sparrow, and the thick-billed king bird have decided to stay and no longer migrate. They have, as is said in meditation practice, "found their seat." They are well-situated between heaven and earth.

And the sun rolls west across the mesa. It momentarily revives the archives of the earth, a Papago hammerstone, a fossil arthropod, fossil pollens from plants that dinosaurs fed upon, footprints of fathers carrying their children, of women scraping meat from the bones of mammoths; where once roamed mastodons, and antlered giraffes, giant ground sloths, the native wild horse and camel, and the great American lion, all more or less silent since the death cry twelve thousand years ago in the Pleistocene.

The sun passes history on the other side of the mesa, dropping down at Freeman's Springs, where the tracks of a mountain lion lead into the unseen-and-only-imagined. The sun casts a thousand little pyramids from a thousand idle stones. The old prayers—Amen to "the hidden one," to Anubis in the cat sleeping in the window and the cat listening, to Isis and Ka—come out when the sun gets low. Their song is too soft to quite make out. But the chant in the bones is too deep to forget, it is the slow repetition of the sound some say was present when that first substantial lightning hit the primal sea and shocked life into existence, the primal sound of being, *OM*.

The word *Om* has been tossed around by people who most often just need a friend and, having rejected God and not-God, don't even trust the root of themselves. Om was the first monotheism, and for the keen of eye, for the beauteous, the great blue heron came next.

Ra turns edges purple and crimson. The bowl of fire is passed on to the western peoples, to the birds and animals waiting through that coldest of hours before sunrise, before night falls from their plumage.

Oak is pierced by the setting sun's last long rays. Tarantula and red ant, lizard and scorpion are touched in the stalks of flowing grama grass. Ringtail cats and road runners, rabbits and rattlers all glow in the vast fiery sweep of sky.

The sun's fire sinks behind the Santa Rita Mountains, and volcano-magenta clouds rise, fire behind the camel's back. The mountains recall their creation. Every cell of stone and rock follows too into the old song, reminded by sun flares that we, too, are created of mist and fire.

That all is Sanctuary.

35. AN ANIMAL METTA RETREAT

THE BUDDHA SUGGESTED that wandering monks should convene in monasteries for three months each year during the rainy season, decreasing the number of insect beings trod upon, while reinforcing the monks' practice. The three-month retreat is still a very viable form of deepening introspection practiced in monasteries and meditation centers around the world. It is a period of "hard practice" in which continuity of awareness is strongly emphasized.

In the last week of September, with temperatures falling well below freezing, we brought the wild two-month-old kitten, rejected by its mother in the empty chicken house, into our home. The dogs, Rottweilers long accustomed to "their territory," were profoundly disturbed and attempted almost immediately to dispatch the kitten.

Barricades were erected, the house bisected between lethal canines and a frightened kitten with an uncanny way of sitting itself on our hearts whenever possible, including under the covers throughout the night. It was like a warm hand on the heart, and we soon began referring to the kitten as "Maharaji's hand." It was not a difficult connection to make because the effect, the states-of-mind engendered, the love inherent in the cells that registered so light a touch from so great a center caused us to continually remember.

But it was difficult to sleep with that purr-engine running over the heart. It required surrender and an ongoing recollection of priorities. Only love truly matters. And the loss of our quiet home: "Your practice is fit for quiet, is it fit for disturbance?!"

We felt our anger rising at the dogs' periodic lunging, growling, and barking at the presumed-temporary children's safety gate across the hall which we had to replace with a securely-installed iron gate. Our quiet home was truly disrupted.

Normally, we might perhaps have simply found a good home for the kitten and been returned to our precious stillness and uninterrupted sleeps. But the opportunity to surrender a bit of our holdings into the priorities of the heart, to take a few months for a metta retreat, were just too obvious to ignore or reject. We had the time and space even to be sleep-deprived if necessary, and we had the tools to cultivate the soft-bellied patience required.

There was a continuity of purpose developing, a subtler sense of compassion for all involved, a committed letting go of momentary resistance, a melting of holdings. A three-month loving-kindness retreat.

It is said that weariness is one of the greatest hindrances to clarity, and thus a useful test of spiritual practice. It's difficult to hold up the mask with one hand and the shield with the other when our body/mind has muscle fatigue. Only the unfamiliar truth remains, with so few synapses left unguarded that we can hear Hieronymus in the next room scraping canvases for his final vision.

It was never truer that love is the only rational act than it was when we surrendered into love, "Maharaji's hand" on our hearts, or sleeping with his paw on the back of my hand as I moved the computer's mouse.

When love becomes the priority and mercy and awareness are the consecrated ground on which the play unfolds, timelessness may ensue. And there were long periods of Big Heart, when I noticed, while reflecting on those people long since out of my heart, that they were found there at my center, and I loved them! Or more accurately, I was in love with them. I was in that place of forgiveness and love so that anyone who approached, I was literally "in love with."

Big Heart embraces all sentient beings. It is the common medium of interbeing.

That year, around Christmas, which is just about the time when the "three-monther" retreats are letting out at monasteries and meditation centers around the world, we offered our precious cat to a friend.

36. THE COYOTE WOMEN

T HE COYOTE WOMEN WERE TALKING in
the woods last night.
They seemed lonely and excited.
Long ago, unhappy, I thought they were
complaining about their husbands.
Now it seems they speak only of God.

37. THE MOCKINGBIRD STORY

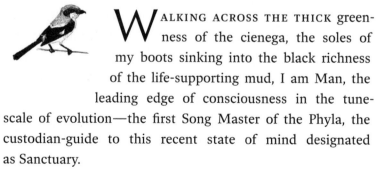

W ALKING ACROSS THE THICK green-
ness of the cienega, the soles of
my boots sinking into the black richness
of the life-supporting mud, I am Man, the
leading edge of consciousness in the tune-
scale of evolution—the first Song Master of the Phyla, the
custodian-guide to this recent state of mind designated
as Sanctuary.

The rains were just beginning to fall in mid-July when we
heard the frightened squawk of a fallen nestling. Beneath the
apple tree, in the midst of thunder and an increasing downpour,
a wet scraggly week-old mockingbird chick was hopping about
while its mother swooped above, unable to return her lost babe

to the bulky nest of twigs and weed stems so well-hidden we could not find it.

First, we took the bird inside. Then, thinking Mother Mockingbird might find a way, we waited until the intense rains had abated and returned the chick to its finding place. On the porch a few hundred feet away, we watched through binoculars while the mother attempted to feed and shelter her offspring from the inevitable darkness and the prowling of countless natural enemies, those who would seek this bird for their sustenance—the skunk, the snake, the hawk, the badger, the coyote, the ringtail, the bobcat, and all the unknowns waiting in some drying niche or nest, with their stomachs growling in wind- and rain-drenched hunger. Mother Mockingbird could only attempt to bluff away these fellow wildlings in hopes of her chick's survival. She might stay through the night, swooping and pecking as she did at our dogs when they sniffed out the babe nearly an hour later, when we returned to see if the protection of our house and our care might not be of greater aid.

Finally, we put the frightened nestling in our daughter's unused playpen to spend the night in a room of its own.

The first afternoon, nothing—the nestling sat in a corner, the milk-soaked kibbled dog food and seeds refused.

The next day we spent much time together, sitting in that bare room squinting and cocking our heads at each other. Then the nestling's irrepressible desire for food broke through and the bird was sitting in my palm, its beak cranked wide open, a funnel cheeping and *tchacking* at me to supply the necessary sustenance.

The mockingbird is a plagiarist, one of the "mimic thrushes." An extraordinary linguist, he often orchestrates the songs of other species into an original creation of the first magnitude. *Mimus polyglottos*: strong-legged, long-tailed, yellow-eyed, with a black, slightly recurved bill. Food: beetles, grasshoppers and other insects, fruit, grape, and holly preferred. That's protein, water, calcium, vitamins.

That second day, perched on my finger, he accepted very lean hamburger and whole wheat bread with his up-tilted wide-open beak. Then, some bananas and more water-soaked bread; then more hamburger. Hotdogs were wisely refused. Plums, peaches, a commercial fledgling food of seeds, eggs, and grains were all accepted heartily. He showed a preference for chicken and bananas, water from his own cup, a piece of moist red-purple plum, an ironic bit of turkey stuffing, breads made with stone-ground flour.

By the end of the week, we were waking with the sun to the insistent *tchacking* of our newest tribal member, who was up, requesting breakfast and fresh water. Our eleven-month-old, wide-eyed daughter Tara would reach up shyly to say good morning to this gray-white fluffy brother. Each day there was a growing communication, with the Mocker flying to the door to greet me as I entered the Bird Room with fresh food—no lon-ger staying in the playpen, now able to fly to his favorite roost atop a wide-mouth stained-glass apothecary jar on the win-dowsill. I sat alone with this growing seven-inch-long fellow being, talking quietly to him as he flew from his roost to the top of my head, jumped down onto my shoulder to peck play-fully at my long hair, and made a new, very low chuck-chuck-ing sound near my ear. He was taking me for a mate. "He prob-ably thinks he's a human being. Or that you're a mockingbird," a visiting ecologist from the Nature Conservancy said one day.

There was a real communication coming about between his bird soul and my human soul; we were addressing one another directly, finding no real difference.

Because our three-month-old, dinosaur-footed shepherd pup is named Li Po after the drunken God-visioned sixth-century Chinese poet, we thought that the Mocker might be named Tu Fu, Li Po's sober-minded court-poet contemporary—for no particular reason of characteristics. A week later, our friend Patricia, writing a letter to a friend, called the bird "Tofu," which is word for the Japanese beancake—a more apt name which stuck. Beancake and I immediately accepted its ironic reasonableness.

By mid-August, Beancake was fat and flying well. It was time for him to go out and follow his genetic directive. One Saturday morning, when we awoke with the arrival of our first visitors from the greater family of San Francisco, having intended to let him back into the sky on that day, we discovered that Beancake was already gone: He had escaped through a space at the bottom of a weather-beaten door which the puppy Li Po had broken through in his drunken, playful attempts to meet this distant birdfellow.

Outside, the dogs sat like spectators at a tennis match, watching the bird fly between the roofs of the two adobe buildings, pushing against the greatest expanse of air he had yet known, his wingbeats perhaps a bit more rapid than need be, more like a dove than a gliding night songster, *tchack-tchacking* to us of his liberation. Free, at play, though still in communication, he flew down to the ground to hop about us chuckling, then up onto the roof, then back to the ground near us, then up to the roof, then onto my head—balancing, stretching his wings, flicking his rudder-tail.

He came into the kitchen with us for breakfast, then went back out into the oak beside the house. When we came out onto the porch, he was sitting on the porch roof, peering down over the edge at us, fluttering down for food and recreation several times during the day. Within a few days, he was following our hikes down to the stream or out on a photographic expedition, flying from tree to tree above us, coming down to sit in the open-topped viewer of my double-reflex camera, chuckling and obstructing my view. Then he would ride home with me down the hill, a great lazy bird in a conquered camera nest, waiting for a raisin or two from my shirt pocket, then he'd head up into a tree to do a tail-balancing act like an oriental fan dancer and warm himself in the yellow summer sun.

By the end of the week he was knocking on the window for food and lodging, dropping out of a tree onto the heads of astonished visitors to chirp for food and have his picture taken, or to sit quietly for a moment if that head should belong to some unnamed good vibration who might *tchack* back at him. He would land sometimes near the dogs, but always keep one hop ahead of them; he was quicker than they, but he had many solo hours still to be logged before complete survival maneuverability would be attained.

Soon there were times when the Mocker flew off by himself to chase his instincts through the trees. Occasionally, while sitting in a tree, he would cock his head to eye a genetically reminiscent insect, pecking at it and trying to swallow this "uncivilized" food. He was growing in his natural aptitudes, though filled with the thought of man as his benefactor, and vociferous and open in his trust.

PART 7: END GAME

While Beancake learned and remembered, the Bird Room was reoccupied by the wounded Cassin's Kingbird: an individualistic bird often seen harassing hawks and ravens above the stream, its family named *Tyrannus* for its fierce personality. The Kingbird's polished ebony eye glistened with fear and defense. His shiny black bill would bite me hello as I placed him in the protective playpen, and he was unwilling to take food until just before his final dull-eyed death.

With the Kingbird laid to rest came the passing of some part of us. The Mocker did not follow the funeral cortège but stayed on the porch, flying over to the apple tree from which he had fallen five weeks before.

On Wednesday night, the Mocker asked to be let in the house. He stayed in the again-vacant Bird Room for the first time in five days.

On Thursday morning, Beancake ate and left for a while, returning in an hour or so for food and the continuance of the ongoing family scene. That night, because we were bidding our visiting friends goodbye the next morning, we decided to drive to Tucson for a farewell supper at a favorite restaurant. On Friday morning, when we arose, the Mocker was nowhere about. We have not seen him since.

Our minds have never been so absorbed in any single recollection. Each bird is observed more closely than ever before; every tweet and whistle is computed against the steady possibility of recognition. We feel like parents listening for a child's voice in a crowded room.

One day, just before sunset, a Cooper's Hawk swooped low above the house and the fear exploded that the hawk may have carried off our friend the evening before. The experience of talons ripping my flesh recurred before and during sleep; the talons wrapped about me, burning into my chest as they lifted me screaming from the ground, the great predator's head turning toward me like an Aztec priest to tear my heart from my body.

Our first experience upon rising each morning is keenly listening for the Mocker's *tchack*. There are the orioles, cardinals, flycatchers, the acorn woodpecker, but no mockingbirds. All day I listen, reflecting, while pulling juniper fence posts from the body of the cienega, freeing her to return to her more natural course. I am utterly absorbed in this absent member of the family, our link with every other sentient creature was included in our miraculous union with the Mocker, which occurred and passed away so quickly. Transience. Attachment. The impermanence out of which all sorrow is born. The very real suffering that the mind brings forth in response to unfulfilled desire.

The next day, too, no Mocker. My mind found the most steady concentration it has ever experienced on the thought of this bird—a total absorption, a one-pointedness never quite achieved in my meditations. The thought-form of this bird is as clear as an apparition. There is an astonishing ability to associate the missing bird with every object or flash of movement, reminding me of God-graced Ramakrishna's comment that if one thought steadily of Christ or Krishna for three days he would find Him. But what of the constant thought-recollection-desire for this slight bird? Would not a meditation on Christ or Krishna be a better use of this mental activity? Yet the magnetism of this bird continues, like the planet's effect on a compass or a holy mountain's effect on a pilgrim, an awkward, often painful steadiness of the mind that will not be shaken, much like that of Tibetan *tanka* scroll painters who will not look at any other images but those which it is their life's work to reproduce over and over, dakinis and demons, bodhisattvas and buddhas, heaven and hell.

There is, I think to myself, the possibility that the bird may have flown off to find its life in the world of birds—a comforting alternative to the intermittent talons of fear. Or he may be molting silently nearby. Or he may have been chased off by his parents when they saw he was able to get about, an instinctive tern territorial defense. There is a great irony in the fact that this bird's instinctual reactions were considerably distorted, by his having taken humans for parents: his song, usually reserved for territorial threat-chant or mating call, become for him a love- and chow-call to his strange biped companions. He may well have been simply misunderstood by his species, an outsider in the bird world.

On the fourth day, the ear and eye found a new modulation, a new awareness born of a new experience of all that soars and flutters, chirps and calls. There came an insight into the passing nature of the lifestuff, into the ten thousand forms of the One, divided, decorated and painted, gilled and feathered, furred and clawed, the Planet Family of which we are all members. And I recalled a story about a great sage who, upon death, was passing from his body through the realms and bardos of the Other Side; upon reaching the top of this final journey, just as he was about to get off the karmic wheel, he thought of a forest doe he had been tending and wondered of its welfare, and was immediately reborn as a deer.

For the past two days, Tara has been looking up into the air, following an unseen flight from sill to table to rafter above my head. It is all too easy to believe she sees that bird's spirit. She has not done this before, and she dearly loved that bird, and would sit entranced for long intervals watching him eat or fly or roost, holding out a flat, self-conscious palm for him to land upon, even letting him rest on her bald head the day before he disappeared. She smiles sometimes at the ghost overhead. Maybe she sees that fellow above us, no longer hungry, though still around in mutual attachment, yet to pass on to some un-touchable world. Or perhaps she sees our intense thought-forms, our desire for Beancake's safety.

Today there was a great gathering of birds about the house: woodpeckers, sparrows, finches, warblers, and flycatchers. It was an extraordinary day, with life-consciousness fitting like a dome over the sanctuary. The initiation has been completed of undertaking our responsibilities as planet stewards.

38. THE TEN THOUSAND NAMES FOR THE ONE, BIRDS SING THEIR WAYS

 AT FIRST, WHEN I CAME to the sanc-tuary, the names of the birds sounded strange and even jocular to my ear: goat-sucker, kittiwake, ferruginous hawk, flam-mulated screech owl, clapper rail, scaup. A ru-fous-sided towhee sounded like a World War I fighter plane to me. Then I came to recognize, in the sounds of birds' names, a mantric quality, a chant-like intonation invoking the freedom of flight and the organic.

Gradually, I also heard in the names of birds their songs. Birds sing in response to their inner states; their songs are as involuntary and natural an expression of mood as a happy man humming or a sad man sobbing. Often, too, birdsong is the expression of the mood of the flock in much the same way that humans' laughter or sadness is carried on through a group—it's an emotional contagion signaling a state of mind. The sounds became clearer to me: great blue heron, varied thrush, phainopepla, ruby-throated hummingbird, night hawk, rough-winged swallow, purple martin, meadow lark, merganser, grebe, cormorant, chickadee, avocet, lazuli bunting. Each sound emanates like the wind through the trees, like a species of its own. Each sound transmits a mood in color and form. As it is said in the ancient Upanishads, the energy of the One is divided into the forms of the ten thousand, and here we see it reflected in the myriad shapes and colors of birds. Like a single shaft of light refracted through a prism, each species takes separate form in sound: whimbrel, sanderling, marbled godwit, crossbill, roadrunner. Each creature takes on an aspect of the universal, each winged being takes flight like a thought grown to a state of mind, finding its niche in the greater mind manifest as planet. Plover, petrel, stint, solitaire, dove, olivaceous flycatcher, arctic warbler, cactus wren, acorn woodpecker, yellow-shafted flicker, anhinga, cedar waxwing, weaver finch, widgeon. Each state of mind is a bird with its own particular reality.

Of all the wildlings, except of course for the insect brotherhood, birds are the most often seen. They exist everywhere, from the Antarctic to the North Pole. They vary in color as much as flowers do, and for many of the same reasons. Birds, like humans and few other warm-blooded creatures, are visually oriented, and what's more, they sing. Their chants reach us everywhere. In the city, their flights raise our eyes from the pavement. In the suburbs, many birds find harmony with man: the cedar waxwing sitting drunk beneath a berry-filled pyracantha shrub by the back door; sparrows quarreling at a feeder; a barrage of juncos flying from the oaks into the flower garden; the ever-present jay policing the bird population; a sparrow hawk following a car down a back road, sampling the insects chased from the roadside grassland; the mockingbird singing through the night to lighten our dreams; the grackle and the blackbird meeting on a golf course to discuss the world of feathered forms; the robin prospecting in the backyard, serenading a man as he lies in bed, conjuring the coming day.

And as the world's climate changes, these feathered minstrels extend their range so that each year we see more and different species which somehow survive the home gardener's pesticides and the developers' million-acre-a-year habitat destruction, though eagle, condor, pelican, prairie chicken, passenger pigeon, and others succumb to man's predatory lifestyle. Across the sky, which shelters us all, are geese and ducks; on the seashore, gulls, sandpipers, herons, and coots grace our life with their individuality. Birds display possession without ownership or murder; they teach us song and architecture, how to dance, and how to fly.

39. VULTURE PEAK

IN THE TIBETAN BUDDHIST TRADITION, many are given a "sky burial," with their corpse exposed to mountain vultures. The corpse's bones are scraped down to offer up the remaining flesh and broken to expose the marrow for the hovering vultures. It is a case of spiritual recycling.

Every spring I have to disentangle once-familiar bird songs from my aging brain cells. I used to be able to recognize their nests and their flight patterns across the riverbed of the cerebellum, but now it's just a guess.

Our most revered non-singing fellow, the vulture, is one of the first to arrive each spring, soaring on the winds. Our vultures return around the Ides of March, which is all very Shakespearian, as they live on the nexus between life and death, on the fertile tideland of impermanence. Vultures are angelic, too, so driven by concern for the wellbeing of Gaia, Earth, that they remove much that might breed illness to sentient beings. The scientific name for the turkey vulture is *Cathartes aura*, which means "golden purifier." The vulture is a promise that hardship, too, is impermanent and often serves a higher end. It is said that in Buddhism the golden purifier is mercy and compassion.

In the tribal communities, the process to which carri-on eaters are committed is very reminiscent of the tribal practices of the Eater of Impurities, a shamanic ritual often practiced on the summer solstice. One after another of the group approaches the solitary shaman, who says, "Give it to me!" and the individual pours forward some hindrance that is blocking his or her heart, or some shame or hidden fear; indeed, the pouring forth may even entail vomiting, the physical release of this mental toxin. Each person is so relieved to be unburdened.

When time and space allowed during our longer meditation-oriented grief workshops, Ondrea and I would often reserve an afternoon outside in some open area or meadow and, with the group in silent meditation, we would invite anyone who wished to approach us to "give it to us." Much of the exposed material was of a sexual nature, as one might imagine; some of it was humorous, some of it terrifying. Many had held in their rock-hard gut a different burning secret, the kind that William James, as I recall, called "the worm at the core." Acting as the Eater of Impurities, we tried to replace what had been each person's brutal self-judgment with mercy in the exposed open wound, and to send loving kindness into their secret wound, to wash us all in the Ocean of Compassion.

And some of these "secret impurities" that were given to us were so very touching because of the absolute innocence from which they were offered. One eighty-year-old woman approached a bit faster than most, so ready was she to release this terrible gnawing at her heart. "I ATE THE COOKIE!" she blurted out. And she told us of a moment when she was nine and her sister was seven and she had snatched a still-warm cookie from a freshly baked sheet of them, and when her mother was angry that someone had stolen a cookie, she had blamed it on her younger sister. She said she thought it had affected their relationship to this day.

She said she was going to call her sister after the retreat and start by saying the same thing to her that she had just confided to us. That day was a good day on Vulture Peak. To be a sacred vulture is a wonderful job for those who have a taste for it. But the hidden grief we all carry is really up to ourselves to begin to relate to with mercy instead of with our usual violent self-ridicule.

The vulture is said to be the forbearer of the Thunderbird, a high totem in the spirituality of many Native American tribal peoples. Some theorize that the Thunderbird myth was based on sightings of an early evolution of a prehistoric vulture-like creature, the *Teratornis merriami*, which may have been accurately described at the beginning of the twentieth century as having a sixteen-foot wingspan capable of flight, but probably favors heavy winds to facilitate lift off, and may well have been encountered by early Native American tribal peoples.

The present-day turkey vultures, "ye ol' buzzards," blithely circle on up-drafts off the ridge; from Cerro de Colorado and Red Hill they come in threes nearly every year to fly over the houses dispersing blessings. The Thunderbird is said to reside on the top of a mountain in the service of the Great Spirit—on the crest of Red Hill, we presume. It is said to carry messages from spirit to spirit.

The vultures tell us the spring spirit is wicking up through the soil. They tell us to live well before they clean us up. We bow to their return. They have so much to teach us, being that they are the only carnivorous bird that does not kill. They are like the panda bear, who does not eat flesh and munches bamboo with sharp teeth, or the bats, which some scientists at the sanctuary were tracking and which stopped eating insects and became pollen eaters. And the vultures are also like human vegetarians who crack nuts and husk hard veggies on their incisors.

After venturing forth from under the Bodhi Tree, the Buddha with his enlightenment well in hand, traveled and taught, settling for a time in Deer Park, after which he traveled and taught on his way to Vulture Peak, a small mountain just outside the ancient city of Rajgir, India. Here, sixteen years after his Enlightenment, he set forth the second Turning of the Wheel of Dharma. Over the next dozen years, these teachings included the world-renowned chant *Prajñāpāramitā*, of which it is said the Heart Sutra is essence and to which the Diamond Sutra attributed the awakening of many, including Hui Neng, the Sixth Zen Patriarch.

40. IN AN UNFINISHED OUTHOUSE IN A SPRING WOOD, COYOTES AND BUDDHAS VISITING

 IT'S THE FIRST DAY OF SPRING, and the snow has melted enough to get down the trail that leads to the *kuti*, the meditation cabin, in the deeper woods below the house, beside the seasonal stream. Ryocan, sweeping the snow from his little porch, nods as we enter the sleeping room.

First, a fire to warm the winter cold that hibernates on the tables and stove, between the pages in the books, and here and there in the pictures. The vaguely mold-smelling quilt that longs for the high mountain sun is hung up on the line, on which also hangs last year's prayer flags, pale and tattered from winter. Their woodcut-printed words and sometimes celestial animal protectors were faded considerably by the winter winds and blowing snow. Their mantras and prayers litter the piney woods.

Inside the outhouse with no walls, which sits near the bend of the seasonal stream, sheltered near the foot of three giant ponderosas, sitting on the boards next to the "throne," just in case there is not enough scenery to entertain the restless mind of the sitter, where magazines might be, there are three palm-size rocks for the "reading." Each, collected on walks, is visibly and tactually unique: garnet flecked with mica, pink quartz striated with a kind of green slate, orange granite studded with white granite. As I sit, inspecting the library of the stones, I am startled, indeed as startled as they are, when three coyotes break from the oak-pinion tree line fifty feet away. We are momentarily the complete occupant of each other's mind. Then they turn and bound up the hill as I, unmoving, dissolve into awe as my heart bows (even from a sitting position) to the bright "animal magic" streaking through their genes.

In mottled shadow, it is all too easy to slip into the dream of some heavy, old animal-headed god and forget the gods of light, of awareness, which create it all.

The puma has leapt up the rockslide to the top of the "cerro" and become sky.

Walking in the woods, I find bloodspots, torn fur, and splintered bone and all, but nature is still kinder than man. The coyote follows the rabbit; the mountain lion, passing through, checks out the buffet. Patience follows fear, opens to it, swallows it wholeheartedly into its deeper nature.

There is so much mica here that we often find pot shards in which the Pueblo potter has mixed crushed mica into the gray clay. On big moon nights, all the mica in the ground and the jutting rock formations sparkles like a thousand moons. It reminds me of that moment beside the dying teenager's bed when I felt her lifted into peace by what appeared to be the Mother of Mercy. When I, a bit too rationally, queried the heavens, asking how could one being, one personage, be present for so many in need, and was answered, "When a thousand people look at the moon, there are a thousand moons." And now, in spring on the mesa, a thousand moons reflect the one. Thoughts arise and dissolve like tiny moons trembling on the ocean of consciousness.

Sitting quietly within the miracle of awareness—even in an unfinished outhouse—we become the light by which we see. Seldom mistaking ourselves for our reflection in the shiny objects that float by. Meeting each one equally with clarity and mercy. Noting detail all about, and within, us. Not confusing ourselves for the contents of the boat of consciousness that passes through on the ocean of awareness. Recognizing we are not the objects of awareness, but the awareness itself, the light by which these objects are known.

This vastness at the center beckons us yet deeper into wisdom, and compassion is the Unnamable to which so many mystics throughout the ages have referred. It is both our birthright and our *unbirthright* because it is said by some adepts that we were born to discover we are the unborn, the essential suchness from which creation springs—like Jesus and Buddha, whose remarkable births remind us that we are born of the Mother of Us All, the endless flow of being into Beingness.

41. STONE, TOO, IS ALIVE

WITHIN STONE, the Precambrian fire still torments the tendency to crystallize.

A stone mason and a poet have the same job, laying stone on stone, word on word. They build hundred-year foundations, they hold the fire safe in our living room and kitchen, they maintain a proper relationship between our food and our fire, they support the roof, and they mark the edge of our world. Some build up stone cairns for the traveler so they know that even if they are momentarily lost they are not alone. These are the functions of both stones and poetry.

Words placed hand by hand, like the New England flat stones discovered along the edge of the territory, create our natural laws. They tell us how far we can go and how wide is the universe.

Molten rock flows up the magma chamber and out the top of the world. Time is in no rush and turns the liquid fire to cool stone. Some mystics say there are entities behind rock facings that mercy can call forth. It is the hidden part of ourselves: the intuitive wisdom, the innate seeing, that knows best where to discover the diamond edge of the heart.

In the cold caldera of time, the fire has subsided, and fossils purr in the stone. Creation has filled our vents with sea foam. Something is wriggling in the cells. Lightning, the heart, has fused with ocean, the body, as consciousness crawls on its elbows from the sea.

Barnacles stud lava coils, brittle black glass thrown from the furnace luminesce in the white moon. Things are boiling to the surface. The eye drops beneath. The ear follows the resonance in the stone echo chamber of prehistory.

Some stone nodules turn the world inside out—these are the geodes whose mild-mannered exterior belies the amethyst forests within.

You can tell when you hold a piece of jade or jasper to your ear that we don't have much time left. The fossils are already beginning to shrug off their captivity.

There are flowers blooming that have not for millennia. Some knew Mary singing, and Mother Sarada Devi forever blessing. Some were carved or drilled to formally hold the heavens. Some were carried in the pilgrim's pocket, or left on our father's grave. It is the fire captured in the strata the makes stones "precious."

This fire tries to save us, but it is too late. We have taken birth in a pile of stones. Our hands are amethysts to hold the fire of healing.

Our legs are river boulders. We are a crane atop our body.

Our body is a rock outcropping.

Stones, like words, can be quite small, yet sometimes spark when one rubs against another.

In water and wind, we begin to wear smooth. This gradual rounding of our edges brings meaning, as is the heart's wont.

Love sets loose all meaning.

At the bottom of an aquarium, the smooth stones slowly tame the water. The cretaceous sun, sequestered in layers of ancient molecules, begins to sing to the fish. It is their chance to warm their blood, to practice evolution. Most swim toward the castle. A few float quietly close to the source.

Moses was promised there was an ocean sequestered in stone. But Moses struck the boulder and broke the bargain with the deluge; he had to pay old Noah's bar tab for us all. Near the beginning of history, in Exodus, Moses needed only to speak kindly to the stones for a cool drink from a warm boulder in the wasteland.

But a few chapters later, a disillusioned deity needs more assurances. And it took some foul language and a goading from his sharp staff to reveal the headwaters of the Nile, but bitter waters confine us to our sorrows. It takes the sweet water of mercy to slake the inborn thirst in all sentient beings, and win back confidence, to crack the rock and break the drought.

The nightingale's diaspora from Egypt crosses many centuries, and lands on the page. It pecks at the rock of which we speak and begins to imitate evolution in a manner that awakens crystals. The first time a few words, a mantra or prayer, sufficed. But on the way to Jericho, it took more than friends in high places and Moses raising his staff to the origins of stone for war not to begin and another drought to occur.

I am drawn back and back into the core of the Earth, where poetry remains molten and unwritten, quietly from phrase to phrase, upward from heart to mind like a light reaching through to the old farmer who watches his land breathe, clearing another field and leaving behind a wall, a New England poem of gray green rock and pastel stone that will live so much longer than he.

Sitting around the stone fire pit by the Paleolithic fire, it was difficult to tell the difference between the runes of language and smooth river rock.

Year by year, the stonemason and the stone become one. His hands no longer belong to him. They have given in to Creation. Homes of stone pour out between his calloused fingers. He does not pray while he works; the touch of stone is enough to remind him

42. SWANS, GRADUAL AND SUDDEN

 "**S**PRING COMES AND THE GRASS grows by itself."
She wants to know when the weather will change,
when the migration will renew our senses?

As an example of winter, she says there is a lake up in the mountains
on which the swans play chess with the clouds moving across the mirror. Carp leap from between the eyes with insights into the gambit,
but fish live forever so it is difficult to tell when they are telling the truth, and which one.

The Gardener-Mother said, "Look after my daughter while I'm gone," and disappeared, taking the seasons with her. Rumi said for the person who loves the truth, who is a friend of God, fire is his water. That person has made spring out of winter; he has learned from his mistakes.

The swans drink from the mirror and fly down to fill the rivers
with slippery silver and glistening salmon.

The swans fill the lake with the likes of themselves that have flown up into the mountains, bringing the sky with them. In the blizzard of their wings, clouds drift out from under the prayer cloth of their long white flight feathers.
When the swans open their operatic wings a star-map unfolds, offering a path—a migration route, really—across the snowscape of small mind's sparse spaciousness.
Murmuring in the next room, they promise not to give us more than we can let go of. A long white wing feather floats into our dreams.

Oh, the upkeep!
Feathers slide through the machinery of perception and dreams soar across the face of the world.
Before the swans came, it was a pretty slow news day.

43. BUDDHAS MARK THE RIVERBANKS

 AH, YES, GARBERVILLE and the south
fork of the Eel River
behind the house where fish-fin divots hatch
owl-eyed salmon fingerlings, swimming
backward to slow the swift waters,
heading toward the sea, following the leader
through treasure-laden canyons
through the symphony of ridgeback whales
through fading shafts of light,
turning toward the calling in their cells,
the call to return years later to spawn
and die where they began.
And the great blue heron who stalked them in his shadow,
and the raccoons that ran the river banks,
scavenging for what remained.
Banded kingfishers drop like spears
into the Eel while the Buddhas
and babies of us all are struggling
to be born from moment to moment,
and dying again, here again,
loosely in human garb.
Disguised as human and heron, as river and rock,
we turn toward the sea
we drift downstream.

44. GEESE CROWD THE SKY LIKE DEVAS

GEESE CROWD THE SKY like devas.
　　Koi congregate in a mossy pond,
　　they nibble at our fingers and
　　tell our fortune. Their beauty
　　convinces him they are real
and were not just pushed out
of the tip of his pen; he drifts
thinking he is God, into Hell,
where he is no longer mistaken
for the real thing and is delighted
to free his body from the great
fear that gave it birth.

45. A DROP OF POND WATER

A DROP OF POND WATER
　　under the microscope
　　just like in science class
　　but now you are the pond
　　and the microscope is mindfulness

ANIMAL SUTRAS

I

Wriggling creatures follow the edge
of the world, their world, a world
without an axis, that does not turn
but pulsates rounded like the eye
that observes...the convex eye explores
the bend in the cosmos through bent glass.
(Is this the wisdom door of "the observed is the observer"?)

Seeking a way out of what imprisons it
and gives it life: the paramecium's quandary.
In the round circus of the drop, Medusa furtively
seeks the forgiveness of the unborn. The shores
of amoebic islands continually advance and retract
in the tiny currents that hold their shifting shape.

II

Examining up through the microscope the curve of the retina
the vermillion fish of fear glisten in the shallows
and dives into the depths to return disguised
as "a practical concern for damnation,"
and an unrealistic distrust
in the moon undulating in the waves.

Passing through the retinal screen
Wish and dream riding over and sliding under
each other, shape-shifting along the long nerve

to the cortex creating the perjury of perception.
Well behind the drawing board, telegram-like impulses
relay the well-edited bundles across synaptic ravines.

Like salmon jumping waterfalls
on the specimen slide, the whole herd of us,
wriggling and whirring. Whirling like moths rising
from flame thoughts that flutter up and perish,
no life shorter than a thought's.

The pond of the usual eye
feeds the fish and birds that shelter there;
the ocean of the inner eye
on which my little blue skiff bobs
from which wafts love and unending praise
of the "open secret" that bends the drop
and the eye and the world in precisely
the same manner following the same arc.

There is no microscope, there is no drop
or pond or eye, not that they do not
exist but that they exist as minutia
in the enormity, the pond in the ocean,
through which we peer to see
in the distance, shimmering down
the tunnel of seeing, quieting
the caterwauling and frenzied prayer
that attempts to escape the "molecular adhesion"
that formally holds form in place.

A few throw themselves against the watery dome
to see what lies beyond—
floating in and out between the eyes.

Having been born of swamp gas, the surface of the mind
covered in floating duckweed, having condensed from mists,
we are all that is left of Creation. The rain that fills the
footprint
that pollywogs unsuccessfully inhabit, the trickle that finds
the pond, bringing with it all the gritty history of its crossing
open ground, a film of dust disguised as kinetic art crosses
the great waters. Mimicking amoebas (or Arp's palette) the
pond ignores
the art critics. We are pond water and a shocking insight
about gravity and fire....and the miracle that breathes in
unison,
rising from the pulmonary moisture, leaving nothing
behind. Securely in the drop, we are allotted and share with
all that.

46. DRAGONFLY

SUNSPOTS ARE LILY PADS,
Buddha a dragonfly.

Remember the first time
You saw all four wings working in unison. The
fourfold way

Curving its body to tip touch the mirror surface. Eggs for
the eons to come
And below, the tiny fish rushed to catch the eggs in their mouths
Removing generations a split second after and before.
It was a hell of a day
But nonetheless
Dragonflies were hatching.

47. QUICKSAND

I F YOU ARE STILL A BUDDHIST or not a
buddhist,
   If you are still a jew or not a jew,
      If you are still a hippie or not a hippie,
         If you are still a catholic or not a catholic,
If you are still a revolutionary or not a revolutionary,
If you are still wise or not wise,
If you are still smart or not smart,
Then how will we ever get out of the box, one box or another,
balancing on the middle way

If you still love god/allah/ahura mazda or don't,
If you still think you know or don't,
If you think your farts still sound like heraldic trumpets or don't,
If you used to love, but now you don't,
If you never loved and now love's about all you are good for,
If you still think in terms of perfection rather than liberation,
. . . . quicksand

48. CAT'S PARADISE

C AT'S PARADISE
    full moon, tall grass

49. DADDY LONG LEGS

D ADDY LONG LEGS FLOATS on agile stilts across the sink onto the long faucet and pranams to a drop of water . . . the delicate world we rarely notice and so easily destroy . . . a tiny flea slaloming through the hair on the forearm, a wind breaks it against a dark hair, it hangs broken as if on the cross . . . the long-legged ballet continues across the sink and disappears one leg at a time into eternity . . . I wash my hands, a swirl of gray matter in the sink and in the brain pan . . . in the delicate world we must hold hands or lose each other.

50. A ROTTWEILER STORY

LAST NIGHT AFTER READING a manuscript about another spiritual sect that called itself "the only way," Ondrea dreamt of toilets overflowing and we awoke to find our Rottweiler, sick of belly, had shit on our *zabuton*, our meditation cushion. (Because, it might be said by someone less refined than myself, "It smelled from years of ass.") He would have gone out if he could but the doors were closed for the night and finding no other acceptable alternative he pooped where he thought he must. It was the only way. And we thought we heard a robust laugh from some celestial's unmitigated heart.

ABOUT STEPHEN LEVINE

POET, DHARMA TEACHER, and companion to the dying and the bereaved, Stephen Levine embodied his own exhortation to "keep your heart open in hell." Born in 1937 to a secular Jewish family, Stephen spent his adult life exploring, practicing, and sharing the traditions of the East, weaving a tapestry of seemingly disparate but ultimately harmonious elements of bhakti yoga (the Hindu path of devotion) and Vipassana (Buddhist mindfulness practice). He died in 2016 in the home he shared with his beloved wife and co-teacher, Ondrea, in the mountains of northern New Mexico.

A longtime friend of iconic spiritual teacher Ram Dass, and of the pioneer of the conscious dying movement Elizabeth Kubler-Ross, Stephen shifted the cultural conversation around death. By embracing both dying and grieving as opportunities for awakening, Stephen and Ondrea helped countless beings approach their own deaths as the ultimate spiritual experience and their bereaved loved ones to be blessed with transformation. Among Stephen's many books, *Who Dies?*, *Unattended Sorrow*, and *One Year to Live* endure as classics and continue to serve as vital guides to those seeking support for navigating the mystery of the human condition.

In their work with both the dying and the living, Stephen and Ondrea reclaimed the concept of "mercy" as an essential element in self-forgiveness, enabling people on a conscious path to leave this world unburdened by guilt, and to dispel the legacy of shame in the hearts of those left behind. These teachings, though simple, were revolutionary. Stephen's book *Becoming Kwan Yin* draws on the Chinese Buddhist bodhisattva of compassion as an exemplar for this liberating practice.

For several decades, Stephen and Ondrea lived in relative isolation in the high desert of rural New Mexico (where Ondrea continues to live), raising children and animals, in close connection with the land. Their solitary life in the wilderness made their outpouring of loving attention to the dying and the bereaved possible. One of Stephen's lesser-known passions was his deep connection with animals, both domestic and wild. A consummate storyteller, Stephen conveyed his relationships with dogs and horses, his encounters with snakes and skunks, and his visitations by mockingbirds and hummingbirds with the artfulness of a bard and the insight of a Buddha.

—*Mirabai Starr*

DATE DUE

THE BLUE TRAIN

Lawrence Clark Powell

With an Afterword by Henry Miller

CAPRA PRESS : SANTA BARBARA

Copyright © 1977 by Lawrence Clark Powell
All rights reserved.
Manufactured in the U.S.A.

Cover: "Gare St. Lazare" by Claude Monet.

Library of Congress Cataloging in Publication Data

Powell, Lawrence Clark, 1906-
The Blue Train.

I. Title.
PZ4.P882Bl [PS3531.0954] 831'.5'2 76-54947
ISBN 0-88496-073-0

Capra Press
631 State Street
Santa Barbara, CA 93101

This is a romance, intended to be to the novel what the string quartet is to the symphony—more compact, chromatic, evocative. It plays variations on a single theme. If it should be thought that actual persons were portrayed, even though it had been so meant there could be little resemblance. Time alters reality, filtering it through memory and imagination, so that what remains is the magic of being young in a foreign land, unburdened by the weight of living that comes later. If Life once sounded discordant, Art has here rendered it harmonious. What then was agitated is now serene. The dedication is to Henry Miller, old friend and encourager.

I

Nancy

O n a Friday afternoon of a cloudy day in early November, the wind from the northeast, I stood on the station platform ten minutes before train time, waiting for the 13.36 *rapide* from Paris. I often came to the station late at night when my eyes grew tired from laboratory work, merely to witness the arrival and departure of the express trains that left the capital in the early evening. There was the Blue Train to the Riviera, the Rome, and the Simplon Orient bound for Italy, the Balkans, Athens and Istanbul. For the price of a 50-centime ticket I could gain entry to the platform and watch the trains make their brief stop for servicing.

This time was different. I was bound for Switzerland to what promised to be a romantic rendezvous. I was already excited as I walked up track from under the high ironwork shell that arched over the boarding area to where the freight yards widened out. They were congested and noisy with the crashing of shunted cars. Brakemen were gesticulating and shouting to drivers of the small engines.

The main line was clear, all lights green, the high rails gleaming as I watched for the *rapide* from Paris. Then I heard it approaching, heralded by a shriek of the engine's whistle; and there it was, bearing down with the overpowering majesty of the black and green, copper-banded P.L.M. locomotive, cleaving the confusion of lesser equipment with the authority of the crack flyer, two hundred miles out of Paris, scheduled to pause only long enough to take on coal, water, and passengers.

I stood back and let the long train pass and then halt with a sigh of relaxing air brakes, before I followed it back into the station. I found my car next to the rear *fourgon*, a black Swiss coach with red and white Maltese cross and placard on its side, reading "Paris-Berne via Dijon, Pontarlier, Neuchatel."

I boarded the second-class end of the carriage and looked for a smoking compartment. All were full. Even the aisle was

8

crowded. I found a jump seat in the vestibule next to the door window, and there I settled down for the journey to Switzerland. I could hear outside the seemingly disorganized uproar of a French train departure; and yet, precisely on time, the shouting ceased and the train rolled out of the station, gathering speed along the banks of the Burgundy Canal, through the stucco suburbs and past the signal tower where a division occurred, one line going down the valley of the Rhone to Lyon, Marseilles, and the Riviera, the other branching off to Switzerland and Italy.

We followed this latter and were soon in open country, running fast over the plain that stretched eastward to the foothills and mountains of the Jura. I did not relish the four-hour journey on the hard seat, and to distract myself, I unfolded and read for the nth time a letter—a letter from a girl I had never met, and curiosity about whom was leading me to Neuchatel.

"Dear Jack," it read, "Your letter was wonderful. You must come. I need you. I haven't been able to find a place for you to stay. My French is hopeless and no one speaks my kind of German. Can't we leave your bag at the station and walk around till we find a room for you? It's not a huge town.

"I'm such a child it's ridiculous to react so vitally to unfavorable health and I think and hope I'm wrong that I have something simply awful the matter with me. What it can be to cause me to lie awake every night I really don't know. I hope you will.

"Please Jack, you will come, won't you? I can't abide one more weekend surrounded by chattering black uniformed French-Swiss jeunes filles. If you don't come soon I'll have to go home although I'm not expected until Christmas. The school doctor speaks and understands nothing but French and I with only English and German, really it's quite hopeless. Why did I ever come here? This is the most urgent plea of my life and funnily, it's not because you're my girl friend's boy friend's former roommate and someone from home I can talk to or a former med student who can possibly help me, but honestly because in a way it's you, the you of your letters. Am I hope-

9

lessly incoherent?

"I know you are terribly busy with your studies and all but it's awful to think there's a sane reason for your not coming. I wish you would let me wire you the money. I've never spent my allowance. I feel like a sick little cold little timorous yellow dog (did I hear you say bitch?). You will come Friday afternoon? I'll meet you at the *gare*. This is amusing, my crying out for help but so I am.

"Your needful, Nancy Clary."

I put the letter back in my pocket and mused over its contents, as the plain began to undulate into the first hills, and the bare trees be darkly interspersed with pines and firs. I would miss only the Friday laboratory. There was a *rapide* back on Sunday evening. I was curious about Nancy Clary, a student of the pipe organ, and said to be both beautiful and rich. And it was my first visit to Switzerland. It was called playing by ear. Would we make harmony or discord? I had no money to spare and would not take hers. It had been long since I had known an American girl. I was susceptible and yielded, and now the train was speeding toward a denouement. I dozed.

Pontarlier was the point of no return. From there most of the train went on to Geneva and through the Simplon Tunnel to Italy. My Swiss coach was coupled on to a waiting train drawn by an electric engine, and soon we were climbing through the last range of the Jura Mountains that separated France and Switzerland. Snow lay on the ground and clung to the branches of the firs. Crows flew up as the passing train disturbed them. Deep below in narrow pockets of the mountains were isolated villages, their houses plumed with chimney smoke. Here and there among the conifer forest, autumn-fired deciduous trees burned in shades of red and yellow. Then we crossed the frontier at Vallorbe, and soon were switchbacking down to the city on Lake Neuchatel.

I saw her on the platform as the train came to a stop: windblown blonde hair, expectant face, thin, worried and frowning, wrapped in a gray tweed coat. I went to her as she came along the platform.

"Thank God, you've come!" she said, as we shook hands in

continental fashion.

"Did you sleep better?"

"Not really. But I think it was excitement over your wire. Do you have more baggage?"

"Just this one. I'm not coming to stay. Let's find a place for me to sleep."

"I already did, just this morning. It's a *pension* room near here. I wish you would have let me pay for a hotel room."

"I can't afford to be in your power. A *pension* room is the limit of my budget."

"You'll let me take you to dinner."

"Where?"

"A perfect place on the lake front. I've already booked our table."

"Bart said you were bossy."

"He told me about you, too."

"I hope so."

"That you are a rebel."

"What else?"

"That you left a brilliant record at med school in San Francisco to bury yourself in a lab in the dreariest of provincial cities. Dijon must be frightfully ordinary."

"I suppose it would be for you. I am working and happy."

"Do you know any girls?"

"What kind of girls?"

"Girls you make love to."

"A different one each night."

"Bart said you were misanthropic."

"A love affair takes time. I've been busy."

"I warn you, I'm not going to have an affair with you."

"That's not why I came."

"Why then?"

"Because you asked me to."

"Do you always do what women ask you to?"

"When they are as blonde and beautiful as you are."

"Flattery will get you nowhere, Jack Burgoyne."

"I suppose it was really curiosity that brought me to Neuchatel."

"I have never known how you came by your last name."

"My paternal grandfather was French, named Bourgogne
When he emigrated, he anglicized it. It means Burgundy."

"Is that why you chose Dijon?"

"Subconsciously, perhaps, but really for the endocrinology
laboratory I'm working in. It has a wide reputation."

We chatted in pauses of climbing the steep street back of
the station that led to the *pension.* At its door we turned and
looked down on the terraced town, dropping to the lake. The
sky was cloudy, the lake colorless, the Alps veiled.

"It's supposed to clear," she said, "and be milder. We're
going on a picnic tomorrow."

"With the school?"

"Heavens, no! Just the two of us."

"Will I be safe?"

"Silly."

"Will you promise to stop frowning? You're getting a
permanent wrinkle."

"It's worry. You must help me."

"I'm not a doctor."

"You'll let me tell you my symptoms?"

"For dessert."

"Don't tease me. I'm serious. I'll call for you at seven-thirty.
You'll have time to change. I don't suppose you brought evening clothes."

"I don't have any."

"It *is* a chic restaurant."

"I have a dark suit on under my overcoat."

"I already tipped the headwaiter and told him we must have
a quiet table where we can talk. May I dress?"

"In black."

"Bart said you were not to be trusted."

"A platonic affair will be a restful change."

"Don't count on anything more from me."

She went off down the steps and I settled in a large room
with wash basin and wardrobe, and undressed for a nap. She
posed a challenge. Was it really only for advice that she
wanted me to come? The answer lay in pressing all the way.

Except for the frown and a brusque way of speaking, she was a lovely girl, although the heavy coat had concealed her figure.

A few minutes before seven-thirty I stood in front of the *pension* and waited for her. The sky had cleared. The stars glittered. Leaves from the plane trees rattled along the cobbled street. The air was sweet with woodsmoke. Below and in both directions were the lights of Neuchatel.

Then I heard a horse and carriage toiling up the street. It stopped and the driver swung down and opened the door for me. Nancy Clary was in the back seat. I got in and sat beside her. The driver wheeled, set his brake, and we went back down the hill, the horse's hooves ringing hesitantly on the cobbles, the brake shoes grinding on the iron-rimmed wheels.

"I have never ridden in a carriage," I said.

"I know you are going to help me. I just know you are."

She grasped my hand. I held hers. She withdrew it.

"I can't help it," I said. "You smell good. You and the woodsmoke."

"The townspeople lit fires in your honor. Do you like my perfume?"

"I thought it was you."

"Bart warned me."

"Can I help it if I'm responsive?"

"I've heard that before."

"So you know about men!"

"I'm no virgin, if that's what you are trying to find out."

"I wasn't, but I'm glad to know."

We reached the lake front and the horse began to trot along the avenue that followed the quay. We drew into a brilliantly lighted garden restaurant at the water's edge.

"Will you ask him to wait?" Nancy whispered to me.

"You mean through dinner?"

"Of course."

"I heard you were rich."

"I am—although the news from home is not good. Daddy says that the Depression is getting worse."

I did as she asked, and followed her into the restaurant. The headwaiter bowed and showed us to a corner table overlooking

the lake; and as we gave up our coats and were seated, I saw Nancy's approving gaze.

"Did you expect me to be in corduroys?"

"Bart said you were unconventional."

"I wouldn't be here if I weren't."

"Thank you for dressing nicely. After all, we are a civilized people and should live that way."

"You talk like an old lady."

"I *am* twenty-five."

"And beautiful."

She was—in a low-cut, bare-armed, black evening gown, her hair done up and banded with a narrow black ribbon. Her eyes were blue, her lips a bit too thin.

"Do you like me?"

"If you'll stop frowning."

"But I'm worried."

"Stick out your tongue."

"I'm serious."

"I'm beginning to realize it. Can't we eat first? Pleasure before business. I'm starved."

"I'm sorry, Jack. I'll be patient."

"Be mine."

She wrinkled her nose at my pun.

Nancy had ordered the dinner, and it was a good one: filets of lake fish sautéed, with a local white wine, chilled and naturally sparkling, followed by *chateaubriand aux pommes frites* and watercress, and a bottle of Romanée.

"In your honor, Monsieur!" Nancy toasted, when the queen of the red Burgundies was served.

The food and drink made me expansive.

"Now, tell me your troubles, poor girl. Why can't Nancy sleep o'nights?"

"That's not it. That's not my real trouble, although I *might* just have a loathsome disease."

"You look disgustingly healthy, like a Swiss milkmaid."

"Horrible thought."

"Tell me."

"It's sex."

I laughed. "*That's* no trouble."

"Stop being so predatory."

"Men naturally are."

"Please listen to me." I went on eating and drinking while she talked. "I've known only two men. An English boy in Cheltenham and an Austrian man in Salzburg."

"As lovers?"

"Yes, but Jack," and she was almost in tears, "I never felt anything. Aren't I supposed to?"

"Normally."

"I've never—what do you call it what you have an orgasm?"

"Never come."

"I've tried so hard to. At first I blamed it on Roger, he was so young. Karl was a man though and very experienced."

She stopped, her eyes tearful.

"What happened?" I encouraged her.

"He cursed me. He said I was a blonde American bitch, as cold as the Arlberg Glacier."

I laughed.

"And you aren't?"

"It wasn't funny. I was never so humiliated. I loaned him money, too."

"And he never paid you back."

"How did you know?"

"I've read the classics."

"You keep making fun of me."

"After a meal like this? You're a marvelous cook."

"I hate to cook."

"Of course."

"What's wrong with me, Jack? Why can't I come? Don't all girls?"

"It's probably psychological."

"What do you mean?"

"You're too self-conscious."

"How do I go about forgetting myself?"

"It's late to start trying, if you haven't learned by now."

"Can you help me?"

"Do you want me to try?"

"No, if that's what you mean."

"You amuse me."

"I'm Irish, I warn you."

We listened to the string orchestra.

"Do you know what it is?" she asked.

"Yes."

"What?"

"Grieg's *Holberg Suite*."

"Bart never told me you were musical."

"I'm not. My mother was. She was a singer and a poet. I learned from her to love poetry and music. My father was a practical man."

"I came here for the course in pipe organ and found the Maître had gone on a tour. A young organist is in charge. I think he wants me to sleep with him."

"Well, why don't you?"

"I've suffered too much of a trauma."

"Didn't you ask me here to make love to you?"

"I did not."

"Why then?"

"For advice."

"You make it hard for me to help you. I might as well go back to Dijon."

"Not till Sunday, please."

"Will you stop frowning?"

"I'll try."

"You spoil your looks when you frown."

"Am I pretty?"

"Beautiful."

"Do I still smell sweet?"

"As all Burgundy."

"O Jack, I want so much to be normal."

"Let me hold your hand."

"Mother told me not to. She said the road to ruin began with holding hands."

"It's not a dirt road."

And so we held hands across the linen, and the meal ended harmoniously. As she was due in at eleven, I suggested that

16

the driver take her home first and then deliver me.

"Take this," she said, handing me a wad of francs. "Please pay for the meal and the carriage. Don't overtip, though; they don't expect it here in Neuchatel."

It was no place to argue. I took the money, paid the check and left a generous tip.

The driver had blanketed his horse, and he was great-coated; their breaths made frost on the air. The night was even sweeter with woodsmoke; and in the carriage, as we rolled smoothly along the lake front, Nancy's fragrance went to my head.

"You may leave your arm around me," she conceded.

"And kiss you?"

"Just one."

I was astonished when her mouth opened to mine and she relaxed in my arms.

We were at her school too soon.

"I said just one," she warned, as I sought to kiss her again.

"Tomorrow?"

"I've planned an outdoor day."

"I'm a great outdoorsman!"

"Meet me in the market place at nine-thirty," she said. "The driver will tell you where it is."

The concièrge opened the great front door and she slipped in and was gone. I paid the driver there, after getting directions to the market place, and found my way back up hill to my *pension* through drifts of wind-blown leaves. The night was cold, and I walked fast for warmth.

I was early for the rendezvous in the morning and wandered about the stalls. The foodstuffs were displayed with Swiss care and elegance—game, poultry, fruits and vegetables, breads and cheeses and sausages. The scene was bustling yet orderly, unlike the disorder of a French provincial market. The forecast proved true: it was a clear day of mild sunshine. The Alps were almost unreal, silhouetted against the pale sky.

Nancy found me in the throng. Again we shook hands.

"I slept!" she said.

"I lay awake."

"Thinking of me?"
"Thinking of it."
"You are a lecherous man."
"And you are a beautiful woman."
"Do you like me in this?"
She was wearing a tan skirt, a green flannel shirt, her hair in a loose knot at the back of her neck, green wool socks and ankle-high boots.
"Who wouldn't?"
"When you wrote that you wanted to walk in the autumn woods, I went shopping."
"I like women in skirts. They're more vulnerable."
"It's chamois—and so am I! You'll never catch me."
We packed her haversack with gruyere, ham, rye bread, and grapes. I slung it over my shoulder, and we set out for the *funiculaire* which took off from the highest terrace. A short steep ride brought us to the mountain top, high above city and lake, the woods at our back. A dirt track led deep into the colored fire of oak, chestnut, and ash; the last leaves of the year drifted around us like butterflies.
"This is my first real walk," she said. "We must not go too far. I'm not terribly strong."
"Is this the road to ruin your mother warned you of?"
"You'd better forget last night."
"That meal?"
"You know what I mean."
"Haven't you forgotten how to forget yourself?"
"I did, didn't I! But we really can't, here in Neuchatel. It's a very proper place."
"Aren't we beyond the city limits?"
"I'm not going to let you, so there."
"Well then, let's take it out in walking."
Toward noon we were passing a farmhouse, and I turned in and bought a litre wine-bottle of warm milk from a roomful of dung-booted peasants. They were gathered around a table in an open shed, husking a mountain of chestnuts.
We walked on out of sight, turned off the path, and while Nancy unpacked the food, I heaped up a drift of dry leaves. We devoured the nutty cheese, the smoky ham and coarse

bread, all washed down with milk, then savored the sugary grapes for dessert. I lay back on the leaves and looked up through bare boughs at the sky, while Nancy took a book from the haversack.

"Do you like German poetry?" she asked.

"Read me some and I'll decide."

"I bought this Insel Bücherei just for your coming. The poems are arranged by season."

"Is there a section called Indian Summer?"

"It is such a beautiful day."

"I didn't bring it with me. Dijon weather is horrible. It's fall, in case you aren't sure."

"Of the leaves, not me."

"You can't seem to get your mind off it. You'll end up giving *me* ideas."

"As long as you don't want to do more than talk."

"But I do!"

"I'm afraid of getting pregnant."

"You can trust me."

"Maybe someday. Could you come to Salzburg?"

"Paris would be the limit of my budget."

"I don't like the French."

"But I am American."

"A persistent one, too."

"Would you like it better if I were a woman?"

"I've never tried it with one."

"You're obviously made for man's enjoyment."

"But not yours, Jack Burgoyne. Please get that through your head."

"Well," I said, resignedly, "If we can't do it, let's read about it."

"I told you these are nature poems."

"Isn't it natural?"

"You're hopeless."

"I trust the situation isn't."

"I'll read you *Oktoberlied*."

"It's November."

"Be quiet and listen."

19

She read beautifully. I stretched out in the crackling leaves, closed my eyes, and listened to her voice reading.

Der Nebel steigt, es fällt das Laub,
Schenk ein den Wein den holden;
Wir wollen uns den grauen Tag
Vergolden, ja vergolden.

"Translate, please."

"It means that in October there is rising mist and falling leaves and someone comes along and pours vintage wine, and the days are made golden; yes, golden."

"Yesterday was gray and windy and last night the world was all flying leaves. We drank wine and voilà; today is blue and gold." I caught her hand and sought to draw her down beside me. "O Nancy, your eyes are lake blue, sky blue, your hair is yellow gold, golden yellow."

She pulled loose. "Unhand me, varlet."

"Milk always makes me mellow."

She laughed. "You are an entertaining guest."

"Read me more, Miss Iceberg."

"Just don't call me a you know what."

"Don't be one and I won't."

She read Storm and Goethe, Rilke and Georg, and as I listened to her soft voice in the strange tongue, I heard only the music and not the meaning. I mused on what she would be like if she could forget herself. It did not seem hopeful. There was not time enough. And I was not patient.

I must have fallen asleep. When I opened my eyes, Nancy was asleep beside me, no trace of frown on her thin face, her breathing deep and regular. I leaned over her on my elbow. She opened her eyes and frowned. The spell was broken. I stood up.

"En route, mademoiselle," I said, helping her up.

We walked slowly back out of the woods and again looked down on the terraced town and lake and across to the Alps, rosy in the afternoon light. We saw a dirt road leading to terrace after terrace, and instead of taking the *funiculaire*, we decided to walk all the way down. We heard the sounds of

children at play, of barking dogs, tramcars, and church bells striking the hour. Peasant women were gleaning in the vineyards. We leaned on a stone wall and rested, while a gleaner crept toward us along the row. When she reached the end at the wall, she straightened to turn and go back, saw us and croaked, "Bon soir, m'sieu, 'dame. Vous vous promenez? Qu'il fait beau aujourd'hui! Mais dépêchons-nous, il va pleuvoir." She waved toward the Alps and the gathering clouds, then resumed her gleaning.

"I'm so glad we came this way," Nancy said, squeezing my hand.

We kept descending toward the town. The air was perfumed with smoke from burning leaves, rising from many points in town. Nancy began to limp from a tight boot, and as we neared my *pension*, I suggested we stop there and rest. I expected her to say no. Instead she agreed. At an *épicerie* I bought a kilo of Algerian dates and a bottle of vin rosé.

"I shouldn't have come," she said, as I closed my room's door and locked it. "But I am so tired."

"Lie down, and let me take off your boots."

She was passive as I unlaced and removed them and then her heavy socks. Her legs were smooth and white. She wiggled her toes in relief. I wet a washcloth.

"That's heavenly," she murmured, as I bathed her feet.

"Your role's reversed, Mary Magdalen."

"I never walked so far in all my life."

"Drink this." I poured her a glass of wine, and I, too, drank a full glass. We ate dates. I sat on the edge of the bed. Her eyes were closed. I began to caress her forehead and to stroke her hair and neck. Her arms reached up and drew me down, and our mouths met again in a wet and winy kiss.

She finally broke away. I said nothing.

"My skirt will be ruined," she murmured, arching her back. "Be a good Jack."

I pulled it off and threw it on a chair.

"Hang it up, please," she whispered.

"To hell with it," I said, fearing to break the spell. I found her mouth again and she returned my kiss, even more

21

passionately. My hand slid down to remove her panties and again she arched her back.

There came a stern rapping on the door.

"Who is it?" I called.

"The landlady. You have left mud on the hall rug. Kindly remove your soiled shoes hereafter when you enter."

"As you desire, Madame, I shall not give offense another time."

I had gotten up to go to the door, and now turned back to the bed, groaning, "Ah God, the tidy Swiss!" Nancy was sitting up.

"Give me my skirt. I've changed my mind."

I pushed her down. "Change it back."

"I won't."

"I'm going to make love to you, if it's the last thing I do."

"It will be the last thing if you do. Let me up."

I held her down. She struggled silently. I pinned her against the wall.

"Come on, Jack," she said, matter of fact, "you can't make me."

"You've heard of rape."

"What pleasure would that give you?"

"Lots."

"You're an egotistical bastard, Jack Burgoyne, and I hate you. I'll *never* let you now. Please give me my skirt."

I threw it high on the wardrobe.

"Don't do that! It's an expensive skirt. You'll ruin it."

"I'll ruin you."

"You've ruined it all, just as I was giving in."

"Give in again."

"Jack, listen to me, I must get back and change, and there's the concert at 8:30. I bought box seats for us."

"We'll make our own music."

"You tried to get me drunk and you almost did." She turned face down, sobbing.

Time passed. I sat on the edge of the bed and would not let her up in spite of her alternate pleading and scolding. I drank the rest of the wine. I was a little drunk, and disgusted by the

way things had miscarried.

At last I relented. I stood on a chair and threw her the chamois skirt. She slipped into it, unlocked the door and was gone. I looked at my watch. It was ten o'clock. I went to the window and threw it open. The street and walks were glistening. The wind had risen and rain was blowing.

I started to undress, and then I relented, hurried into my clothes, took my overcoat, and went out. She was sheltering under a nearby fir tree. I threw my coat around her and we hurried silently back to her school. I was cold sober, ashamed of having overplayed my hand. While waiting for the concièrge to open, she removed my coat and I put it on over my wet clothes.

"Thank you at last for being a gentleman," she said, coldly.

"At your service, Miss Blondebitch." I bowed and walked away, as the door closed. I trudged back to my room through the empty streets. The leaves underfoot were sodden.

I was awakened in the morning by a soft knocking on the door.

"Who is there?" I called, expecting the landlady to answer.

"It's me, Nancy. Let me in."

I got up and unlocked the door. She pushed by me.

"How did you sleep, Mr. Caveman?"

I did not answer, and began to wash my face and comb my hair.

"I slept," she offered.

"I didn't expect to see you again."

"I came for my haversack."

"It's there in the corner."

"Don't be cross with me, Jack. Kiss me good morning. Or do you insist on shaving first?"

"I'm taking the noon train."

"It's an *express* and it stops everywhere. Please take the 20:30 *rapide*."

"What would I do with myself until then?"

"Be with me."

"What do you mean?"

"What I say."

"We behaved badly."

23

"I'll take the blame, if you'll stay. Please stay. I need you. I've felt so well since you came." She took my hand. "I lost my head when she knocked. Forgive me." She embraced me. I breathed her freshness of hair and skin and soap. "We can go back to our bed of leaves."

"It rained."

"We can stay here."

"What if she knocked again?"

"Keep our heads under the covers."

"This is a new Nancy."

"Don't be cross with me. Nancy loves Jack. Nancy will offer proof of her love if Jack wishes."

"Carnal?"

"Utterly."

"Nancy Clary in the role of Delilah. Instead of cutting my hair, will you shave me?"

"Put on the lather."

We laughed. "Wait for me out front," I said. "I'll shave and dress and be right down."

"Will we come back here?"

"All I can think of now is my stomach. We'll take care of the other organs later."

"I have never known anyone as outspoken as you."

"I can't help it."

"I'm accustomed to more genteel persons, but I'm beginning to like you, Jack Burgoyne."

"I'm willing to start over. Are you going to wait outside for me?"

"No, I want to watch you shave."

"Where will we eat?"

"I know a nice place on the lake front where we can have petit déjeuner."

"I want breakfast, lunch, and dinner. Dates is all I've had since yesterday noon."

"Poor man, Nancy will feed you."

I felt my interest rising as she showed this contrite side of her nature. The day was fair after rain, and it was an attractive outdoor restaurant on the quay, under pollarded plane trees,

the water of the lake all but lapping our table as we ordered a mushroom omelette and ham, bread and sweet butter and jam, with café au lait. Under the morning sun the lake was dancing with whitecaps. Fresh snow had whitened the Alps. The promenade was peopled with the Neuchatelois in their Sunday best. They were a staid folk all dressed in black.

While I ate hungrily Nancy nibbled at her plate; and she, too, was silent until finally she looked at her wrist watch and said,

"You've missed the noon train. I was afraid you might change your mind. Now you're mine until tonight."

"Possessive, aren't you? I must say, though, I like the new Nancy."

"You've done it. I hate myself for panicking. I knew it would have happened."

"What would have?"

"Do I have to say it?"

"Yes."

"I felt myself having an . . . I felt myself . . . coming."

"What was it like?"

"Fire under the ice. I felt myself beginning to melt and flow."

"There's hope for you. You haven't frowned once this morning."

"You don't hate me?"

"You're too selfish."

"So are you. You came just to have a good time at my expense."

"To have a good time together. That way we cancel each other's selfishness."

"I ruined it."

"You'll do it again if you keep talking about it."

"I want more than anything to be normal—and not pregnant."

"No danger with your Uncle John."

"Do you know why I am not frowning? Because I know that something nice is going to happen to me."

"You *can* be sweet, Nancy Clary."

"And we will turn the gloomy days to golden days, yes, golden."

25

"Did you bring the little book?"

"Only my fair young body and my long golden hair."

It went the way she wanted and that I had hoped, the day before, it would go. We returned to my room, undressed, and lay on the bed. She was beautiful and good to love, with no trouble between us and no knock on the door. Somewhere in the *pension* a violinist was practicing Bach sonatas; and as we lay quietly afterward, Nancy hummed along with him. Sunday in Neuchatel was dead quiet. No noise rose from the street. We slept and then made love again.

When it grew dark, we dressed; I packed my bag, and we walked to the station for supper in the buffet.

"I'm starved again," I confessed.

"The stomach is terribly important in your scheme of things."

"I have a rapid rate of metabolism."

"I'm so glad I'm normal. It was so good. For the first time in my life. But I wonder?" She clung to my arm, and I saw that she was frowning.

"Now what's the matter?"

"Jack, are you sure I'm all right?"

"You mean pregnant?"

"Silly! I mean *not* pregnant."

"Of course you won't be. Didn't I explain to you?"

"I know, but what if there was a leak?"

"Should I have blown them up?"

"Don't be sarcastic."

"Then don't worry."

"Women are born to worry."

"Give me one that doesn't and I'll make her my goddess."

"You're not the one who will swell up and be horrid looking."

We had reached the station, taken a table in the buffet, and ordered dinner of roast lamb and white beans and a chicory salad. Nancy would not eat. Her hair began to come down and she went to the rest room to pin it up. When she returned, she was frowning.

"I know you think I'm impossible," she said, "but I really think I'd better go home and take a douche."

"Eat something first. See me off, then take a carriage. You'll be all right. Let me pour you some wine."

"I know you think I'm always spoiling it for you."

"You are."

"And I'm frowning horribly."

"You're not pretty anymore."

"I don't care. I just can't eat. She smiled wanly. "I think I have evening sickness. Please get me a carriage."

"Do you mean it?"

"Please, I must go."

I followed her outside to the carriage rank.

"Get in with me, Jack, and sit a minute. Kiss me good-by."

"You have a genius for ruining things."

"Wasn't it worth it?"

"A thousand times no," I said cruelly.

"Won't you kiss me good-bye?"

"No."

"Will you take this money?"

"No."

"You are heartless."

"Only when you make me so."

"Please, Jack." She began to cry.

I turned away and went toward the buffet door. I heard the carriage door close, the wheels grinding on the cobbles as it turned, and the horse's hooves beginning the deliberate klop klop, as it drove away.

Though full of self-disgust, I ate both portions of the lamb and beans and salad and was on the platform as the *rapide* from Berne came in, silently drawn by an electric engine. This time I found an empty compartment in the through car to Dijon and Paris, stretched out on the wide seat with my overcoat for a blanket, and soon fell asleep to the clicking of wheels over the rail points.

II

Erda

What draws a man to a woman—that draws one man to one woman when they are only two among thousands? In the beginning it was probably because she went bareheaded even in the coldest weather. Her hair was the color of ripening cornsilk. It hung to her shoulders in rippling waves and gleamed in the winter sunlight. She was short and solidly built, with a strong stride. Each noonday when she passed the café window as I was taking an apéritif, I watched her come up the Rue Chabot-Charny, probably from the Faculty of Letters, cross the Place du Théâtre to the sidewalk outside the window where I sat, then on past the Church of St. Michel and out of sight.

She was obviously not French. High cheekbones and aquiline nose indicated what race? Slav? Magyar? Finn? I came to await her daily passage, a kind of princess among the provincial throng that streamed by each day on the way home to lunch; and though I stared at her coming, her passing profile, and her going, never did she notice me.

After she had gone, I mused over my vin blanc-cassis. Should I follow her and learn where she lived? Or block her way and introduce myself? I did neither. I was wary of all blondes after Neuchatel; and yet, though I was occupied in laboratory work, with little free time, I wanted the company of a woman. No Dijonnaise drew me. The sweetness I had tasted with Nancy, although it had turned bitter, was like honey at the back of my tongue.

Then one afternoon, because I was interested in the Symbolists, I went to a five o'clock lecture, given by the Dean at the Faculty of Letters, on Rimbaud, the wonder boy of French poetry. She was there. I saw her a few rows below me in the petit-amphithéâtre. Throughout the Dean's crisp, logical, and elegant *explication*, I stared down at her, seated to one side so that I could watch her face partly in profile, strong yet not masculine, wide, generous mouth, large forehead. She

seemed spellbound, never turning her gaze from the short, dark, fox-like speaker. The hour went by. My mind was divided, following the Dean's lecture and at the same time dreaming of her who fascinated me, wondering how to draw her to me as I was drawn to her.

"Lucid, yet mystical," the Dean concluded, "as in these lines, saying all, meaning what? Take them with you, listeners, as a talisman in memory." He lowered his voice, and read:

> *J'ai fait la magique étude*
> *Du bonheur, que nul n'élude.*
> *O vive lui, chaque fois*
> *Que chante le coq gaulois.*

The applause was loud and long. The Dean acknowledged it with a sardonic smile. The students waited for him to leave the platform, then they crowded into the aisles. I stood at the back, watching her come up the steps; and then as she approached, drawing on her gloves, I took a deep breath, stepped in her way, and heard myself say,

"Je demande pardon, mademoiselle, mais puis-je vous accompagner chez vous?"

Her blue eyes stared into mine, and for a second I feared defeat. Then she smiled and said in English,

"If you like."

"But . . . but . . ." I stammered, "you are not English."

"I prefer it to French."

"You speak it beautifully."

"How nice of you to say that."

"English English, not American English."

"Will you teach me American English?"

"How did you know I am American?"

"I am a wise woman."

"What are you?"

"Do you wish to see my papers?"

"Forgive my curiosity."

"Guess."

"Finnish? Esthonian?"

"You speak like a world traveller."

"Hungarian? Russian?"

31

She shook her head.

"I give up. I only know that you are the most beautiful woman in Dijon."

She laughed delightedly. "I'm an ordinary Swede from Stockholm."

"I am an extraordinary American."

She laughed. "From San Diego."

"How did you know?"

"The nephew of the lady who keeps the *pension* is a colleague of yours at the Faculty."

"Who?"

"Raoul Dupont. He has told me of you, the lone American, the recluse, the woman hater, so regular in his habits, so intelligent and brilliant—a genius *enfin*."

"I thought the Swedes were serious, but you are a tease. What is your name?"

"Erda."

"Erda what?"

"Erda Lindström."

"Erda means earth. What does Lindström mean?"

"It means linden stream."

"I'm John Burgoyne."

"May I call you Johnny?"

Throughout the conversation we were partly blocking the aisle, oblivious of the push and jostle of the students; and it was she who finally took my arm and steered us out onto the street.

It was dark, the street thick with bicyclists, furiously ringing their bells as they rode home from work, candled lanterns swinging from their handlebars. We walked along the sidewalk toward the Place du Théâtre, and when it narrowed, I dropped off into the cobbled gutter. As we crossed the Place and approached the café, she squeezed my arm and said, "That's where you sit at noon."

"You've seen me?"

"Like a fish in an aquarium."

"And I thought I was studying you."

"Don't you know how perceptive women are?"

32

"Sometimes I forget. An apéritif now?"

"I am not supposed to, unchaperoned. Yet I will with you."

We entered the warm, smoky café and sat side by side on the leather *banc* against the wall, under an ornate gilt-framed mirror, with another across from us in which we could see ourselves. The room was rumbling with Burgundian French, over which her English accent sounded exquisite.

"You like poetry," I said.

"Not particularly."

"Why were you there?"

"Madame Décat says that the Dean speaks the purest French in Dijon. He bored me, so logical, like a scientist dissecting a butterfly."

"He looks like a fox that's raided the hencoop."

"She says he has a very bad character."

"Did you see me?"

"I felt you."

"You knew I was there?"

"Why didn't you come sit with me? I thought Americans were friendly."

"My grandfather was French."

"The French aren't shy."

"I'm not very typical anything, I guess. Are you enrolled in Letters?"

"I go for the learning, not for a diploma."

"What are you doing in Dijon?"

"It's called *absorbing culture*. I was in Germany, Italy, England."

"Where next?"

"Home."

"When?'

"In three more weeks."

"May I see you again?' '

"Madame Décat has not encouraged me to have rendezvous."

"She's not running a convent, is she?"

"Madame is strict. Raoul will vouch for you though. In fact, he already has."

"You know more about me than I do about you."
"It is a woman's way."
"How old are you?"
"Guess."
"Twenty-four."
"I am only eighteen."
"You are so womanly."
"We women of the north mature early."
"I have been led to believe that Swedes are a somber people."
"Laplanders and Norwegians, perhaps; Swedes and Danes—toujours gai!"
"You have had men friends here?"
"The Dijonnais do not interest me."
"What do you like to do?"
"Ski. The Côte-d'Or is no place for ski-ing."
"Do you like to walk?"
"Very much. I am strong."
"Music?"
"Oh, yes!"
"Would Madame allow you to go to the opera with me a week from Saturday?"
"Come home with me and ask her."
"And for a walk this Sunday?"
"I'll say yes to all that you ask of me."
Such was our beginning. Erda was extroverted, unsentimental, vigorous, and healthy. We shook hands in meeting and parting, and her grip was as strong as mine. In the beginning we were like brother and sister. She resembled an American college girl in her forthright manner, but with flashes of an exotic foreign cast of mind. I called her my blonde Viking. She did not show any romantic interest in me or in anything.

Our night at the opera changed that. It was a one-night stand by a company from Paris. Dijon's shabby municipal theater across from the café was packed with the town's élite. Erda was beautiful in a sea-green gown which revealed her strong white arms, shoulders, and neck. Her hair was done up

34

in a severe coiffure. She was eye-catching amidst the over-dressed, heavily perfumed throng, and I saw several of my professors stare at her, then wink knowingly at me. I was enormously pleased with myself.

The opera was Moussorgsky's *Boris*, its music passionate enough to overcome such handicaps as rickety scenery, dusty stage, ragged orchestra, an off-key soprano and a restless audience used to Puccini and Massenet. The bass who sang Boris, however, was superb, and the bells of the Kremlin, rung off-stage, were deafening. At the climax of Boris's death, I saw tears on Erda's cheek. Her hand reached mine and squeezed it hard.

As we walked home from the theater, she clung to my arm and was quieter than I had ever known her. It was a clear night, the stars like bright powder, and our breaths made frost on the air.

"You were moved by it," I said.

"Oh Johnny, I never knew music could be like that."

"Hearing it together does it."

"With you, Johnny, with you."

She was transformed from the tomboy I had known before. All my senses were heightened by the knowledge. As we neared the Rue de Metz, our heels ringing on the cobbles, we saw a glow ahead and hurried toward it. A building was on fire. The occupants had fled to the street in night clothes and coats. A crowd stood transfixed, their faces raised like flowers to the fiery spectacle. Firemen were coupling hoses and raising ladders and commanding the people to stand back. No one moved. Blue flames spurted from the metal gutters. Window glass cracked and crashed. The roof suddenly burned through and a fountain of sparks played into the windless sky. The crowd gasped.

We shoved into the thick of it, Erda clinging to my side, and there we stood pressed together, surrounded by people oblivious of each other. Erda began to tremble.

"Cold?" I whispered, drawing her closer.

She did not answer.

I felt my way beneath her fur coat. Her body was hot. She

pressed even closer and whispered in my ear,
"I hope they never get it out."

My own excitement mounted as I realized that the fire had aroused her. I moved so that I stood in back of her and let my hands, still beneath her coat, begin to caress her breasts and belly. No one paid the least attention to us, their faces ruddy in the glow. My lips found her warm neck. My hands grew more ardent. Her breath quickened and suddenly her body went rigid. My arms tightened around her until she slowly relaxed and would have slumped to the ground had I not held her fast.

"We must go," she whispered finally. "I promised Madame I would come home after the opera."

We forced our way out of the crowd and hurried the rest of the way to her *pension*. As she searched in her bag for the door key, I sought to kiss her. To my astonishment she broke free, slapped me hard, and cried, "Let me go." She opened the door and it slammed in my face.

I stood for a moment, then walked home through the empty streets. The wind had risen and window shutters were banging in the still of the night.

A week passed. My puzzlement changed to anger at the way she had reacted. I moved across the Place to the Café de la Comédie for my noontime drink and did not see her pass. Then on the following Saturday morning Raoul Dupont brought a note from Erda, asking me to have Sunday lunch at her *pension* and go for a walk afterward. I told him to tell her yes. I wanted badly to see her again.

Madame Décat was well known in Dijon for her culture. Before she had been widowed by the war, her home was a salon. Now it was an exclusive *pension* for foreign girls. She was petite with gray hair and pale blue eyes and a lovely sad face. Luncheon was formal. Erda and I were elaborately polite to one another. I had no eyes for the other girls, but directed my attention to the hostess. Raoul was in Paris, and except for the butler I was the only man present. Madame Décat led the talk through topics as varied as the comparative sweetness of Spanish and Californian oranges, the preparation of Burgun-

dian snails for cooking, the amount of honey in the best Dijon gingerbread, the limestone formations of the Côte-d'Or, the music of Rameau and the sermons of Bossuet, two of Dijon's most glorious native sons. The talk was lively. She knew something about everything. The food was elegant, and in my honor she opened a vintage bottle of Clos Vougeot, a heady red Burgundy.

After lunch, and the girls had dispersed and Erda was changing into walking clothes, I found myself alone in the parlor with Madame Décat.

"Let me get to the point," she said softly. "You are aware, I am sure, Monsieur Burgoyne, that Mademoiselle Lindström's parents have charged me with responsibility for their daughter while she is under my roof."

"I assumed she must have parents," I countered, "although she has never referred to them."

"Although she obviously possesses some of the attributes of a woman, she is still a girl, and of fluctuating emotions. Since you escorted her to the opera, she has been in a rather high state of nerves."

"Music affects some in this way."

She smiled faintly, then said, "As a student of human nature, as well as of the more exact sciences, you are familiar with the psychology of infatuation."

"I assure you, Madame, of the honor of my intentions. Erda will testify to the platonic nature of our relationship. To speak the truth, I have not seen her since that evening."

"Just so. I know something of your lineage, Monsieur Burgoyne, or you would not be my guest today. But I must inform you, inasmuch as she tells me that she has not done so, that Mademoiselle Lindström is affianced."

"To whom?"

"To one of Stockholm's most substantial financiers. A banker, to be precise, and a widower of an age, it is true, considerably more advanced than hers. A most distinguished individual, I am told, and of great means. She is spending these months abroad at his instance, chaperoned, to be sure, in order that she may prepare herself to be the lady of his house."

"We do not favor such marriages in our land."

"Customs vary, as we observed in our conversation at the luncheon table. One learns tolerance."

"I am not planning an elopement," I protested.

Madame Décat arched her thin brows and shrugged her shoulders. "I am convinced of the truth of all you say. But here is the point my dear young man, here is the point I have taken far too long to arrive at—and I beg of you to forgive my prolixity—I should not care to see your relationship with her transformed into something more ardent. Mademoiselle is young, I repeat, and though fully developed as a woman in body—indeed most seductively so, I am fully prepared to admit—and accomplished beyond the average in such diverse interests as sports and languages, the creature is still essentially a naïve."

"This is indeed part of her charm."

Madame Décat again ventured a small sad smile. "Raoul was right. You are truly not a crude foreigner; so unlike the Americans we are accustomed to, thick tongued and heavy handed. Your perceptions and reactions are altogether Gallic."

"My grandfather was French," I reminded her. "From Auxerre."

"The purest of Burgundian. And you, my esteemed friend, are a very likeable young man."

"Thank you, Madame. What is your price for this fine compliment?"

She chuckled. "Raoul did not sufficiently emphasize your roguishness." Her face hardened. "I will tell you. It is imperative that Mademoiselle Lindström leave Dijon in the same state in which she arrived in my care."

"And that is precisely what?"

"A virgin, my dear son, a virgin."

"But my dear Madame, we have been as brother and sister. We have never exchanged—I hesitate to say enjoyed—a single kiss."

Again she gave me a tired, wise, and compassionate smile, then flared her eyes and said, "This is her last week in Dijon;" and added with icy precision, "I am counting on your honor

Erda

as an erstwhile neophyte of Hippocrates to see that she leaves
Dijon—and may I borrow a phrase from your discipline—that
she leaves Dijon *virga intacta*."

Erda entered the parlor at that moment and I made no reply.
I thanked my hostess for a delicious lunch, bowed and kissed
her hand, and Erda and I took our leave

As we walked through the curving narrow streets and
reached the aspe of Notre Dame, Erda halted and drew off her
glove.

"You must also remove yours," she said, and when I had
done so, she took my hand and placed it on a little owl carved
in relief on the stone of the church.

"What is it?" I asked.

"The wishing owl. See how smooth it is worn?" She put
her hand over mine. "Now wish together." And after a pause,
"Have you wished?"

"Yes. Shall I tell you what?"

"Then it wouldn't come true."

"Tell me yours."

"Guess."

"The same as mine?"

"Yes."

The afternoon was bitter cold and we walked fast to keep
warm, stride for stride, her arm in mine, neither speaking,
until we reached the park on the edge of town. It was about a
mile square and been created in the seventeenth century by Le
Notre, the great landscape architect. The incidental details of
his original design had long since vanished, and there remained only the basic geometrical pattern of unpaved walks
and intermediate groves of ancient trees, now stripped bare to
a company of skeletons. The park's southern limit was the little
Ouche River, and there on a stone bench at its edge we
rested. Although barely four o'clock, the sun was low in the
sky and there was no warmth from its rays. We gathered
leaves and twigs and lit a fire, took off our gloves and warmed
our hands. Crows rose from the stubble field across the
semifrozen river and cawed their heavy way toward the low
sun. The time was winter and everything was numbed and

39

slow. The sweet smoke from the fire rose without wavering.

"Why have you avoided me?" she finally broke the silence.

"Was it because I slapped you?"

"Partly."

"Is there someone else?"

"No."

"I was frightened by my feelings. I have always been sure of myself."

"You were so responsive."

"It was the music and the fire—and your hands and lips."

"I didn't want to let you go."

"All week I have longed for you."

"We are together now."

"Madame Décat would surely reprove me for my boldness, but I must say it. Do you want to hear it?"

"Tell me."

"I love you."

We stood up and I took her in my arms and sought to kiss her.

"No," she said. "You must tell me first what you and she were talking about."

"More about snails and oranges."

"Liar. I saw her face."

"She told me what is going to happen when you go home."

"Oh, I hate her for that! Johnny, I swear I don't love him."

"But you are going to marry him."

"Yes, I am."

"You foreigners have quaint ways."

"Don't be sarcastic. I am going away in another week. Have you thought of me at all?"

"Every night."

"Oh Johnny, kiss me now."

Our first kiss was long and deep and tender, while her gloved hands stroked my face. She was radiant as my hands found her again under her coat.

"I am so happy," she said. "Can we walk again before I leave?"

"Lab keeps me until five every day and by then it is pitch

dark. Can you come at noon?"

"Madame made me promise not to, even with you."

"Evening?"

"I am all but locked in my room."

"She is a veritable watchdog. A pity she has forgotten her youth."

"She has never forgiven life for having left her a widow."

I looked at my watch. "If we hurry, we can hear a concert from Paris."

"What do you mean?"

"Sundays before you came, I always went to a friend's house for the five o'clock radio-diffused concert from the Conservatoire. It won't be like the other night, but I think you'd enjoy it."

My friend was an old French *confiseur* from the Vosges who had retired to a family property in Dijon, a great eighteenth century *hotel* in the Rue Berbisey, where he spent hours huddled over the loud-speaker, tuning in music from all over Europe. He lived alone and welcomed my weekly visit while we sat silently in the formal parlor, listening to the broadcast and nibbling a plate of his sweets, with a liqueur.

We found Monsieur Bonespoir fighting static, as he struggled to bring in the Paris broadcast.

"You honor me to return," he greeted us, "and to bring with you such a charming creature. I must apologize for the cold. I suggest you leave on your coats."

The pink-eyed, walrus-mustached, portly old candymaker had on his coat, hat, muffler, and gloves, while he muttered and twirled the dials and cursed the crackling interference. Then all of a sudden Radio Paris came in bell-clear and the concert commenced with the *Roman Carnival* overture.

"Enfin!" he beamed and brought out a plate of cookies and gingerbread and poured us tiny glasses of kümmel, where Erda and I sat at a great square table, covered with green baize and over which hung a beaded chandelier with one bulb of low wattage.

The Berlioz was followed by a song-cycle for soprano and orchestra, a *première audition* of *Les Heures du Foyer*, a suite

41

of lullabies sung by an expectant mother, seated at the fireside, to her unborn child. It was followed by the *Daphnis and Chloe* music, an orgy of sound that made Erda's eyes shine and her hand reach for mine.

Old Bonespoir joined us at the table during the entr'acte.

"You also like music?" he asked her.

"Oh yes!"

"You must come again with Monsieur Jean."

"Alas, I leave in another week."

"Where do you go?"

"My home is in Stockholm."

"Tiens," he exclaimed, "the other side of the moon."

"You have travelled?"

"Once to Grasse, for a particular perfumed condiment."

The final music was the César Franck symphony. We were carried away on the flood of sonority, holding hands, staring at one another across the table in the dim light.

The concert ended and the old man saw us to the door.

"Did I ever tell you?" he asked me, "that Sophie and Mirabeau occupied these chambers on their elopement from Paris? Your coming here, so close do you seem one to the other, reminded me of those passionate ones." He shook our hands and murmured, "Ah, la belle jeunesse!"

The door closed. We crossed the flagstone courtyard in the biting air and the great wooden street door slammed on our backs like doom. We hurried through the narrow streets that formed the mazy heart of the old town, for it was after seven and she was late. We stood a moment at the door of her *pension*, but when I sought again to reach beneath her coat, she pushed me away.

"I dare not. We must say farewell. Adieu, my love." She kissed my cheek and was gone. I walked away down the curving street, my desire not cooled by the snow that had begun to drift down in the dark.

The days passed. I kept vigil at the café. In vain. Perhaps she had left before the appointed time. Then I learned from Raoul that Erda was still in Dijon and was leaving on Friday. On Thursday all of the faculties of the university were closed,

along with other state institutions, because of the funeral in Paris of a war hero. The day was cold and rainy, and I remained in my room. As the bell clock on the municipal library tolled three, there was a knock on my door.

"Come in," I called, seated at my work table, my back to the door, believing it to be the chambermaid with clean towels.

The door opened and a moment later from in back of my chair cold soap-sweet hands closed over my eyes.

"Guess who!"

"Erda!"

I stood up and took her in my arms. Her cheeks were cold, her lips warm.

"I have longed to see you," I said.

"You sent no word."

"I waited each noon."

"I took another route, pausing each day at the wishing owl."

"I went there one day and wished. And now do we not have our wish?"

"I was afraid. I have promised Madame Décat that it would be our last rendezvous. I hoped that somehow you would find me and then I would not break my promise."

"I despaired, particularly when you parted so casually."

"Oh Johnny, you must not say that! I am not casual. I am a frightened girl. I have never known these feelings."

"I thought you northern women matured early."

"I was teasing you. I will not tease you any longer. When Raoul reported the faculty closed today, I had an overpowering desire to be with you. Promise or no, I came."

"In the wind and the rain. Take off your coat and let me hang it to dry."

"I brought you a present for your little phonograph." She took a parcel from the bed. I opened it and found a recording of Franck's *Variations Symphoniques*. I put it on. Erda looked around my room at books and pictures. She found a bottle of Sandeman's ruby port and poured us each a glass.

"Skaal!" she toasted, and sat cross-legged on the floor beside my chair.

43

I removed her wet beret and her hair fell loosely to her shoulders, silky and fragrant. I whispered in her ear, "Look up. Let me see your face. You are thinner. There are circles under your eyes."

"I have thought of you in the sleepless night. Yesterday while shopping with Madame, I heard this record and I returned today and bought it for you. I wanted us to hear it together."

"My darling."

"I brought you something else."

"What?"

"You might not want it now. How can I say it? "

"Whisper in my ear."

I slipped to the floor beside her and for a moment we were joined in a kiss. Then she freed herself and said,

"It is myself that I bring you." And then, even softer and in French, "Parceque je vous aime. Je vous . . . je t'aime, tu sais."

Again we kissed, but I could not forget our predicament. It was a student *pension*. There were no locks on the doors. People came and went in great informality. The nosy chambermaid was everywhere at all hours.

I lifted Erda up and we went to the window. I opened it and we looked down on the rainy street and across to the wine merchant's courtyard where workmen were rolling barrels across the cobbles to the cellar chute. The lamplighter was making his rounds in the darkening afternoon and stopped beneath us to raise his long, lighted taper and thrust it up into the bracketed lamp which in a moment began to glow with golden light.

"Do that to me," she said, seeking my lips, "Oh Johnny, do that to me."

"We must cool off," I said. "There is no privacy, and besides, we deserve at least a night, not an hour."

"But how? The Décat has become so vigilant. I leave tomorrow. She knows that I love you. I told her so. I want to tell everyone. I wanted to call down to the lamplighter."

The rain blew in on us as we stood together and kissed.

There came a knock on the door and even before I could call "Entrez!" the chambermaid burst in with the towels.

"Pardon," she said, "I was unaware that Monsieur had company." She gave me a knowing look, arranged the towels with elaborate care, and finally went out.

"See what I mean?"

"Play the record again. Music fertilizes my brain."

We stood at the window in a close embrace all through the *Variations*, and then she spoke.

"Would you love me in Paris?"

"What are you saying?"

"Could you join me there?"

"But how? You are going home to be married."

"To a man I love not. That old Croesus shall not have me first."

"But how?"

"I am not supposed to tarry in Paris, of course. Madame is putting me on the train tomorrow and I am to taxi from Gare de Lyon to Gare du Nord and take the Nord Express to Hamburg where my fiancé's agent is to meet me."

"You are booked through to Stockholm?"

"Stopovers are permitted."

"With whom?"

"I have excellent friends there whom my family would trust to chaperone me. A young Swedish married couple studying at the Beaux-Arts."

"Would they delegate the chaperonage to me?"

"I stopped over with them on my way here in October and they were sympathetic to my plight. They would gladly aid me in a deception of Old Moneybags. They would join me in a telegram to my parents, and then you and I could be together for a few days, even for a week, if you did not tire of me."

"A week of nights."

"As you desire. Can you leave your work?"

"I can make it up."

"I have enough money left for us both."

"I have some," I lied, knowing that I would have to borrow. "When does your train leave?"

"The two-thirty *rapide* from Lyon."

"What class?"

45

"First. You must board without her seeing you. She's hardly worried now though. She believes her little lecture cooled you off. I, too, feared that it had."

"Raoul won't give us away?"

"Tell him you've been called to Switzerland again."

"Of course. On banking business."

"Oh Johnny, I want you to have me first!"

"And I want you. Wait and see."

We pledged the rendezvous with a kiss and she left. I leaned out the window and saw her wave as she hurried up the Rue de Petit-Potet.

I went early to the station the next day, taking a back way along the canal path, carrying a suitcase and wearing my overcoat, for the cold had settled down for the winter and the sun was seen no more. I checked my bag to Paris, then gained the platform and walked along in the direction of Lyon out into the freight yards, and there I waited for the *rapide* to arrive, certain that I was out of sight even if Madame Décat should accompany Erda to the platform.

Once again I was going to a romantic rendezvous, but this time in place of the curiosity that was a main part of my motivation in meeting Nancy in Switzerland, I felt mounting desire to be with Erda in Paris and to satisfy the passion I knew she was capable of. Compounding the intensity of my feeling was the excitement of eluding Madame Décat's vigilance and of cheating the old Swedish banker of his interest due.

I heard the *rapide's* shriek as it entered the yards and then saw the huge engine bearing down on me and the long train roll past and come to a stop a few cars up track from where I stood. I boarded the carriage in front of the *fourgon* and remained in the rear vestibule until the train began to move and gather speed. I waited until it had cleared the station and the yards and was running fast along a ledge at the bottom of the limestone walls of the Ouche, before I began to make my way forward from car to car, seeking Erda.

Had she boarded? What if she had changed her mind and taken an earlier train? Or if Madame Décat had decided to accompany her to Paris? It was too late for me to don a disguise.

My uncertainty increased, and the sweat began to trickle down my body under my clothes, as car after car did not hold her. Passengers looked at me suspiciously as I peered into each successive compartment. The train was running at full speed now, swaying on the curves as the line climbed the low hills separating the watersheds of the Yonne and the Seine. The wintry landscape was a blur through the steamy windows. Erda, Erda, darling, darling, I kept muttering, hoping to evoke her. Although I had lost count of the cars, I knew that I was near the front of the train, for I began to hear the locomotive's exhaust, powerful and regular, overtoned by the cry of the whistle as we approached a level cro.sing or flew through a village. The *rapide* was due to stop only once, at Laroche-Migennes for engine water.

And then, when I had nearly given up hope of finding her, I heard my name called.

"Johnny!"

I turned. It was Erda, standing in the corridor of the first-class coach, with an older Frenchman. I had passed by the couple, not recognizing her in a black tocque, veil, tailored dark suit, a fur coat on her arm.

Relief turned to jealousy. How could she be so casual? We chatted a moment. The man regarded me as an interloper, evidently believing he had made a pickup. I grew angry. I saw his face stiffen. Erda intervened. She took my arm and said to the man, "You must say good-bye now. I am to have tea with my fiancé."

He and I bowed stiffly and I began to relax as she and I made our way back along the train.

"There *is* a restaurant car, isn't there?" she asked.

"It is in the middle of the one hundred cars that constitute this train. I had despaired of finding you and then to encounter you in the company of that *cochon!*"

"I feared you were going to strike him. I, too, had despaired of your being on the train, when you were so long in finding me. And so I let that stupid shoe salesman engage me in conversation."

"I thought I would never reach the front of the train, and

then I passed right by you without knowing it."

"Do you like me in this?"

"Lift your veil and I will tell you."

We were at table in the restaurant car. I ordered English tea, toast, and port.

"She suspected nothing," Erda exulted.

"I'll not relax until we have left the Gare de Lyon. She might have telegraphed someone to meet you and escort you to the Gare du Nord."

"It is unlikely. We will telephone my friends from the station and obtain their permission to telegraph my family in their name. They'll think it a charming deception."

I watched her remove her gloves. "Need help?"

"Later."

"You'll want me to?"

"You'll despise my woolen underwear."

"I, too, wear it in winter."

We laughed in relief and anticipation.

It was dark when we left Laroche-Migennes. The lights of villages and farms flashed by. We reached the Gare de Lyon at seven o'clock. It was swarming with passengers, brilliant with lights, noisy, confused. Would there be someone looking for her? I began to sweat again. I waited outside the P.T.T. office while she telephoned and sent the telegram to Stockholm. The Blue Train was beginning to board passengers for eight o'clock departure to the Riviera. The Simplon Orient and the Rome expresses also stood waiting.

When at last we gained a taxi and the porter stowed the bags at our feet and beside the driver and the door slammed and the car entered the traffic flow in the rainy street, I collapsed with relief. Only for a moment. I roused myself and took her in my arms and my hands went beneath her coat.

"We made it," I breathed in her ear. "Now they'll never find us."

"Oh Johnny," she murmured, turning her body to mine.

She lifted her veil. We kissed. Our mouths remained fused all the way to the hotel. My hands roamed over her body.

It was a small hotel near the Place St. Germain-des-Près.

Our large, high-ceilinged room was papered with enormous birds of paradise in red and blue. The first thing Erda did was to open one of her suitcases, dig to the bottom, extract a garment and hold it high.

"I bought it for our honeymoon," she exulted. It was a sheer black silk nightie. I took her in my arms.

"Now?"

"Isn't Johnny going to feed his girl?"

"Do you want to go out?"

"I'm hungry, and besides I want to see the boulevard at night."

And so we walked to the Place and after dining at the Restaurant des Saints-Pères, we moved across to the Café de Flore and sat on the *terrasse* next to a glowing charcoal brazier. I had never known Erda so gay and talkative. Finally she sensed my impatience.

"You want to go to bed, don't you?"

"With you. Tonight."

"Soon."

"Now."

"Isn't it nice to know we can?"

"Then let's!"

A crone hobbled up with a basket of hot chestnuts in cornucopias, freshly filled from her roaster at the corner.

"Buy me some to eat in bed," Erda teased.

Another peddler had stopped, sensing a sale, and I took a bunch of violets from his basket and pinned them on her suit lapel.

"You eat the violets," I said, "and I'll eat the chestnuts. Aren't you getting cold?"

"Poor Californian! At home this would be a mild evening."

"Shall we go now?"

"Will it be like at the fire?"

"Hotter."

"Then I'm ready."

Erda proved a vigorous lover. Her body was strong from sports and it took all my strength to lead in her clumsy ardor. When she finally fell asleep on the torn-up bed, I opened the

window and looked out. Daylight had come. Snow was falling between the high buildings that lined the narrow street. The room smelled of her and me and us and violets. I lay down beside her, pulled the sheet over us, and fell asleep.

Paris in the winter, the coldest winter in years, the city shrouded in a blue-gray veil. The damp air smelled of coal smoke and Chanel. It was perfect weather only for lovers. Erda lived in delight with everything, especially the great department stores where she went shopping every afternoon. I accompanied her the first time, and then we had our first quarrel, when I said that I preferred the museums and galleries. Neither of us would yield and for the rest of the week we spent our afternoons apart, I going to the Louvre, the Luxemburg, Orangerie, Cluny, Rodin, and others I had read of and never seen. I would return to our room late afternoon with a pocketful of postcards, and soon after, Erda would burst in, laden with parcels, throw them on the floor and herself in my arms.

Then we would race to see who could be naked first, flinging our clothes around the room and falling together on the bed. Afterward I would doze and when I opened my eyes, Erda would be sitting naked on the floor, tearing open parcels and exclaiming over each thing she had bought—gifts for half of Stockholm, I teased. She always brought a gift for me—a tie or handkerchief or pen and pencil set, saving my package till the last. She was irresistible.

One day a small trunk was delivered into which she began to stow her purchases. She was like a child at Christmas, gay, responsive, and also willful and spoiled. No quarrel ever lasted for long. She would end by pulling me onto her with Viking passion. Her strength was nearly equal to mine.

Evenings found us in harmony, for each night we heard music together, feasting on riches of symphonies, chamber music, recitals, always half a dozen events to choose from.

The unbroken cold brought misery to many. Along the lower quays men and women huddled around bonfires, grotesquely wrapped in rags and newspapers against the cold. The Métro platforms were peopled with the homeless. In the Rue

de Rivoli I saw a coal-wagon horse fall and snap a foreleg with a sound like a pistol shot.

We were young and in love, bearing Blake's "lineaments of gratified desire," and the suffering of others did not touch us deeply. We saw it and did not like it, but were not moved thereby; if anything, it increased our own self-absorption.

Then one morning, while we were sitting up naked in bed with café-au-lait, croissants, and confiture, Erda announced that her money was gone.

"You should have told me," I scolded her. "I have only enough to pay for our room. The rest I spent on our meals."

"Don't be cross with me, Johnny."

"But you will need money for the station and meals on the train and you're not leaving till Saturday. We must eat and we planned on chamber music tomorrow night, our last night."

She laughed. "Oh Johnny, you are so serious. Don't worry. I'll go see Sven and Gertha tonight. They'll give me money. I must go alone though."

"Why must you?"

"I just must, that's all."

"Was Sven your lover?"

"Of course not. You're the only one."

"Perhaps."

She burst into tears for the first time. "You're hateful and jealous. Why must you be?"

I embraced her. We didn't get up until noon. She had her way though. I spent a lonely evening while she went by taxi to her friends in Montparnasse. Hours passed and she did not return. I went time after time to the window, pulled the flowered drapes and looked down. Snow was falling. Taxis passed; none stopped. She did not come. I grew worried. I tried to phone. No one answered. I began to read a Tauchnitz edition of *Lord Jim*. No use. I stared at the flamboyant wallpaper and counted the birds. The bell in the tower of St. Germain struck the hours, hour after hour, and still she did not come.

It was three in the morning when she finally burst in, laden with parcels, as fresh as ever, excited and laughing.

51

"Don't scold me," she cried. "I have lovely presents, all for you."

"Beware of Swedes bearing gifts," I growled, half angry, half relieved.

"And money," she cried, opening her bag and flinging a handful of paper francs on the bed. "We're rich again."

"Did you sleep with Sven?"

"Johnny, you mustn't talk that way. You know I'm your girl."

"Why were you so long?"

"He insisted we go dancing, and as I'd had a thousand francs from him, I couldn't refuse."

"Why didn't you come and get me?"

She hesitated. "Well, there was another Swede there—a boy I grew up with in the Ostermalmsgatan—and Sven thought it better not to let him know I've been with you all week."

"And so the four of you went dancing."

"Don't be jealous, Johnny, please don't be."

I was not to be appeased, and for the first time we fell asleep back to back.

The morning brought another day. We awoke and turned to one another again and lay abed until early afternoon.

That last afternoon, reduced to just enough money to get her home, Erda let me lead. I took her to some of my favorite places. In the Luxembourg Museum the virility of Bourdelle's bronze Herakles Archer made her eyes shine. We walked through the bare gardens and on to St. Clothilde where César Franck had been organist, and back along the Boulevard St. Germain to the Faculty of Medicine, where I showed her the museum of monstrosities in jars of alcohol. She shuddered and clung to my arm.

We dined our last night at the Voltaire, opposite the Odéon, on trout from the Auvergne and a bottle of flowery Chablis whose bouquet brought pleasure to diners at the next table.

"I like you better poor," I toasted her. "I've had you all to myself since you came home last night."

"This morning."

"And tonight."

52

"Our last night."

"Don't be sad. Be glad I'm marrying a banker."

"Selling yourself."

"I gave myself to you."

"Only for a week."

"You're so serious. I thought Americans were frivolous and gay."

"Is that why you wanted to meet me?"

"Please don't be stupid."

"I want to hurt you."

"You will if you don't stop."

In spite of the food and wine, I was glum, and she gave up trying to amuse me. We took our seats in the Salle Pleyel and waited for the music to begin. We did not speak and did not hold hands. It was an all-César Franck concert, his string quartet and piano quintet. The richness of the strings brought me to life. My hand found hers.

"Oh Johnny," she whispered, leaning toward me, "isn't it beautiful?"

We were reconciled by the music to our differences and our parting. When it was over, we walked back to the hotel, seeing the great department store façades illuminated with animated toy displays for the Christmas season.

"Even if I had any money," she said, "I couldn't spend it. They're all closed."

"Do you want to stop at the Flore for a last drink?"

"Yes, and I have a confession to make."

"You mean you are?"

"I won't know that till after Christmas. Do you want me to be?"

"Would it bring you back?"

"Johnny, listen to me. I've lost my passport."

"What?"

"I must have left it in one of the shops when they asked to see my papers. I can't get through Belgium and Germany without it. What shall I do?"

It was not until we were seated at the café, with little glasses of Remi Martin, that I had an idea.

"Go to your consulate in the morning and ask for a transit passport to Sweden. They have a record of your being in France and will surely issue you one."

"They ought to, but will they?"

"Show me the man who could say no to you."

"You don't know the Swedish functionary. He's as cold as a frozen herring."

"Wear what you did coming up on the train."

"I'll try."

"Maybe he'll refuse and then you won't be able to leave."

"Be honest, Johnny. You'd grow tired of me. Or angry. You're grown up. I'm still a girl. I don't really want to settle down."

"What will *he* say about that?"

"I'll wear him out and inherit his money. Then I'll come to you."

"Mad girl!"

"You don't know how impoverished my family is. They have been living on borrowed money until my marriage is consummated. I'll wait a week, then give him a bag of bills to pay."

"Mercenary Swede. It's a horrible system."

"I don't know any other. You know now, don't you, that it's you I love."

"Are you ready for bed?"

"I'll really show you that I love you."

She did indeed. It was the best night of all. We were utterly compatible. In the fire of her surrender my destructive emotions were burned away. Delight remained in purest essence. And sleep, the deep sleep of complete fulfillment.

We rose at nine after breakfast in bed, and somehow managed to pack her things, loaded all into a cab, and drove to the Swedish consulate. I waited while she went in. I lay back in the cab, beyond feeling, and waited. The lapel of my overcoat was sweet from where her head had rested. She returned, waving a paper in her gloved hand.

"I did exactly what you said. Never lifted my veil. Removed one glove and touched his hand, oh so timidly. He issued

me a transit visa—and asked me for coffee. I said no thank you, my grandfather is waiting for me." She kissed me. "Wasn't I polite?"

I leaned over the driver. He was reading *L'Ami du Peuple*. I tapped his arm.

"Alors, m'sieur 'dame?"

"Gare du Nord."

We arrived half an hour before the Hamburg *rapide* was due to depart, and after checking Erda's baggage, we entered the station buffet.

"There are shadows under your eyes," I said, "as there were that day when you came to my room."

"And for the same reason. Lack of sleep."

"I slept."

"I watched you."

"You were so good last night."

"Have I learned the American way?"

"All ways."

"Oh Johnny, you've spoiled me. You'll forget our quarrels, won't you? They were all my fault."

"Darling."

"Can you make up your work? Will Raoul aid you?"

"I'll work terribly hard to keep from thinking."

"You won't forget me?"

"Never."

"Now may I have a kümmel?"

"That's all I have left. The price of one kümmel."

"Take these francs."

"You'll need them."

"Will you go right back?"

"I hope I can make the eleven-thirty *rapide*."

"Tell the old gentleman I loved his cookies. You'll go tomorrow?"

"Every Sunday."

"I'll be listening." She raised her glass. "Skaal, Johnny." She sipped and handed me the glass.

"Skaal, Erda."

We were in the stream just above the falls.

Then we found her car, a first-class black and red Deutsches Reichsbahn carriage, with placard reading "Paris-Hamburg." Steam was billowing from between the cars. We walked forward just as the engine eased into the coupling with a soft clash of steel.

"You did that to me, Johnny," she murmured. "You did that to me."

We looked up at the gloved driver. He looked down at Erda. She blew him a kiss. "Drive carefully," she said. He looked at his watch. The air was bittersweet with the ancient smell of Paris.

Five minutes.

We walked back to her car and mounted to the vestibule. I found her beneath the fur and for the last time I ran my hands over her body. Our eyes sought the lasting image each of the other.

Two minutes.

"En voiture!" the conductor called.

Erda grimaced and wiped a tear from each eye with her gloved hand. I kissed her with all my might, until I tasted her blood in my mouth.

"Adieu," she whispered. "Good-bye, Johnny."

I kissed her again, as though I could arrest the train by the force of my desire.

Useless. The train began to move. She broke away and pushed me toward the open door. I jumped off and nearly fell. She leaned out and waved. I waved back.

The train gathered speed with incredible swiftness, and in a moment the *fourgon* glided by, faster, faster; and through a smother of steam I saw its two ruby lights, like the eyes of a beast.

III

Joyce

I spent the Christmas holidays in the laboratory, making up the lost week; and to repay the money I had borrowed, I gave English conversation lessons to French students. The cold weather endured. Streets and walks were icy and treacherous. Erda wrote twice, and sent me a copy of *Gösta Berling* in English; and though I answered and wrote again, I heard from her no more.

I was effortlessly chaste. Nothing diverted me from study. I slept late, went to the café for apéritif and lunch, was in lecture or laboratory from two until seven, dined at the *pension*, sometimes went to the movies, then returned to my room and studied and read to music, or joined in a bull session in another student's room, until going to bed long after midnight. I lived on stored-up heat from Erda. She had irradiated me for the winter.

Old Bonespoir had returned to his natal village in the Vosges and there were no more Sundays in the Rue Berbisey. I acquired my own radio receiver, and it brought in the musical riches of Europe from London to Warsaw. At my work table, which was covered with sailcloth and lighted by a lamp with an orange-colored shade, I heard music through earphones, while I labored on a translation into English of an endocrinology text by one of my research professors. Pinned on the wall above my table was a print Erda had given me, of Bourdelle's glowering bronze of Beethoven, its inscription reading, "Moi je suis Bacchus qui pressure pour les hommes le nectar délicieux."

After midnight as the stations began to go off the air, the house grew still and no sounds came from the street; then was heard only the striking of the hours on the town's many bell clocks. For the first time in my life I had broken the sensual barrier and attained a serenity in which my mind was free to flower.

And then one day in early spring when I had finished lunch

Joyce

and was about to leave for the Faculty, a British couple named Penfield entered the café. They were students of landscape design, living in Dijon while writing a thesis on ancient Burgundian parks. I had met them one weekend at Vézelay where we had gone to see the Basilique de la Madeleine. Burton Penfield was tall, thin, and bespectacled, his wife Mildred a plump Irish woman with rose-petal skin and honey-colored hair.

A woman was with them I had never seen before. The café was crowded, and mine was the only table with empty seats.

"May we?" Penfield asked.

"Please do. I'll be leaving."

"Stay," Mildred Penfield said, "and meet my friend Mrs. Davies."

The woman's eyes met mine, and I was the first to look away. Hers were green eyes in a blank white face.

"We've been trying to persuade Joyce to see Vézelay now that she's this close," Mrs. Penfield said, "but she insists on going through."

"To?" I asked, to be polite.

"Cannes." Mrs. Penfield replied. "Have you been to Vézelay again?"

"I've been too busy."

"What occupies Mr. Burgoyne so urgently?" Mrs. Davies asked.

"Jack is a science student at the medical faculty," Penfield said. "A slave to his studies, especially since he was in Paris last winter."

"I do not care for doctors," the woman said.

"Jack would never actually cut into you," Penfield explained. "He's more apt to dissect you philosophically."

"Jolly brilliant, these Americans," Mrs. Penfield said.

"I would not have taken Mr. Burgoyne for an American," Mrs. Davies said.

"Would you like to see my passport?" I asked.

"The Americans I have known have all been rotters."

"One finds what one seeks," I said.

Our eyes met again, and this time hers dropped. She lit a

59

cigarette and blew the smoke in my face.

"Thanks," I said. "I happen to like the *Gauloise bleu.*"

The Penfields were embarrassed. I rose.

"Back to the formaldehyde vat," I said, "where life is less hazardous."

Mrs. Davies smiled faintly. I shook hands with all three and left.

All afternoon in the laboratory her perfume lingered on my hand, an exotic smell soap and water did not remove. I recalled her chic clothes, her long legs crossed high up, her thin face with wide mouth, and above all, her green eyes. I had not seen her hair, for she was wearing a tightly wound dark green silk turban.

I went to the movies that night to see Charlie Chaplin in *Les Lumières de la Ville.* It was the third time I had seen it, enthralled by the master pantomimist and the musical score he had composed for the picture; and I walked up the aisle afterward, humming the little flower girl's song.

Then in the crowded foyer I found myself pressed against— Joyce Davies. She was with the Penfields. When she turned to see who was crowding her, our faces nearly touched. Hers cut like a knife. Only for a moment; then her eyes widened in recognition and I saw that their green was amber-flecked.

"Monsieur le docteur," she murmured, with the faintest of smiles.

"We're going to the Miroir for coffee," Penfield said. "Will you join us?"

"Please excuse me, I said. "I have work to do."

"It would give me pleasure if you would come," Mrs. Davies said in French.

"I thought you didn't like Americans?" I countered, also in French.

"Are there not exceptions to all rules?"

"I assure you of my profoundest gratitude."

"Do come," she said in English, "I'll behave."

A whiff of her perfume decided it. I went with them up the Rue de la Liberté to the Brasserie du Miroir. A string orchestra was playing the ballet music from *Le Cid.* The

Penfields and I got into a discussion of Cluny in southern Burgundy and the merits of Viollet-le-Duc's work, while Joyce Davies listened, watching the face of each speaker, her own veiled in smoke from the strong cigarettes she favored.

"Are you always this silent?" I challenged her, in a lull of our talk.

"Afraid of angering you again."

"Joyce is still fatigued from her journey," Mrs. Penfield explained. "She came across on the Trans-Siberian."

"All the way across?" I asked. "What kind of equipment do they have?"

"Horrible. And the food was even worse. It took two weeks."

"And she wants to leave tomorrow," Mrs. Penfield said. "We are frightfully annoyed with her."

"Go on talking architecture," she said. "It's so reassuring."

She intrigued me. Who was she? Not French, although she spoke it fluently. I kept trying to place the perfume. Was it Chinese? I did not leave early as I had intended to do. It was Monday night and the Miroir and the town's other cafés all closed at eleven.

"Just as I'm waking up," Mrs. Davies protested. "Is there nowhere open that I may stand a round of Pernod?"

"The *buffet de la gare*," I said, "is open all night."

"Shall we go there?" she asked.

"We'd better not," Penfield said. "Jack, you go with Joyce. A bit of night life will do you good."

I did not protest. And so we separated, the Penfields going off to their apartment and Mrs. Davies and I retracing the Rue de la Liberté to the Place Darcy and on to the railway station. We walked silently under an arch of plane trees in new leaf.

In the smoky buffet she removed her coat for the first time and I saw that she was a mature woman, full-breasted, round-armed, thin only in face and shapely legs.

"I see that you approve of me," she said. "I suppose you'll be wanting to sleep with me before the night is over."

I stood up in anger.

"Sorry," she said, taking my hand. "I seem to be fated to annoy you."

"You are accustomed to men finding you irresistible."

"You speak the truth."

"Have you tried not wearing that perfume?"

"I do not wear perfume."

"What is it then?"

"It is on my clothes. Our closets were made of sandalwood."

"In China?"

"Indochina."

"So that is an Oriental mask you wear."

"For protection."

"Take it off."

"Why should I?"

"Where are you staying? I'd better take you to your hotel. We don't seem to be getting along."

Her face softened. She took a long swallow of the milky Pernod. "Please don't." She lit a Gauloise. "I'm beginning to relax."

"Why so tense?"

"The long journey, I suppose. Men on the train annoyed me. There was no privacy."

"I want nothing from you."

"I'm beginning to see that you don't."

"Who are you?"

"You know my name."

"Let's not spar."

"Do you want me to take my hair down?"

"It might help."

She began to unwind the turban.

"I wrapped it too tight. It's giving me a headache."

Her hair came down in a flood, thick and curly and copper red, clear to her shoulders.

I reached out and touched it. "Will it burn me?"

She laughed. "It's all my own. Nor do I tint it."

"Why do you hide such beautiful hair?"

"I attract enough attention without this bonfire."

"It is indeed an incendiary red. Now tell me who you are."
"Please don't be an aggressive American, just as I am beginning to like you."
"Do you dislike all men at first?"
"Mostly."
"I don't suppose I'm any different from the rest. I am just a man."
"That is obvious."
"Why don't we be simple with each other? Dijon is a poor place for melodrama."
"Don't you find it dull here?"
"I do not seek excitement."
"Why are you here?"
"To work. Why are you?"
"Passing through. And to see Mildred. Do you sometimes go to Paris?"
"Not since December. The severe cold burned me."
"Your paradox fails to hide the presence of a woman."
"You are perceptive."
"Tell me about her."
"She returned to the Arctic Circle."
"Tiens, an Eskimo. How exotic!"
We laughed.
"What do you do to amuse yourself?" she asked.
"We were at the movie, remember?"
"Was that tonight?"
"Last night. We met yesterday noon."
"Do you have a girl here?"
"No."
"Lucky you. Was the one in Paris good?"
"She was really Swedish, not Eskimo."
"Where is she now?"
"She went home to Stockholm to be married."
"Lucky you."
The train caller entered the buffet and poured out a torrent of words.
"I thought I knew French," she laughed.
"He's calling the Blue Train. It's due to make a ten-minute

stop. Want to go see?"

"Whither thou goest . . ."

I put fifty-centime pieces in the vending machine for billets de quai and we gained the platform and waited beside the main line until the de luxe sleeping-car train from Calais and Paris came in precisely at midnight. Blinds were pulled on the windows of the blue and gold *wagons-lit*. A mechanic hurried along with a flashlight, crouching to check the journal boxes with a rap of his hammer. A few people boarded. No one got off. The Blue Train carried only through passengers for Marseilles and beyond.

We walked back along the train, drawn by a lighted, unshaded window. There we gazed up. Four red-faced Englishmen in shirt sleeves were sitting, rigidly erect, playing cards. We were so close that I could read the label on their bottle of Johnny Walker. One man looked down and saw us. His lips moved soundlessly. The other three turned and looked. Their faces were expressionless. We stared up at them. They turned back to their cards. The train began to move and gather speed. As the *fourgon* passed us, we saw the baggage-master standing in the open side door, his ill-fitting, red-corded, black uniform open at the throat, in the act of tilting a wine bottle to his lips.

"Santé!" I called, as the car glided past.

His Adam's apple twitched. He removed the bottle from his mouth. "À la vôtre, m'sieu'dame," he said.

Joyce squeezed my arm and laughed.

We walked the length of the platform after the departing train, until finally its rear lights disappeared around a curve. We walked out from under the shell and saw the yard signals turn red. The air was damp and smelled of coal smoke and hot oily machinery. I told her of the last times I was there and of Nancy and Erda and what I had learned from them.

Joyce clung to my arm as we walked in slow strides together and I spoke of my successes and failures. I touched her hair. It was beaded with moisture. The bitter smell of coal smoke blended with her sandalwood. We drifted back under the arch of the station.

"I call it my cathedral," I said. "Shall we eat something?"

"As you like. I seem to be yours without your asking for me."

"You've grown wonderfully gentle."

We entered the buffet and ordered ham and gruyère sandwiches, coffee and brandy.

"In a few more minutes," I said, "the Simplon-Orient is due. And then the Rome. And at 2:38 there's the Bordeaux-Strasbourg *rapide*, the only fast train in all of France that does not originate in Paris."

"I am coming to the conclusion that you like trains."

"I often come here at night to see them pass. If I do not visit the buffet, it costs only fifty centimes."

"I thought I never wanted to see a train again."

"Now tell me—are you an international spy?"

"Heavens no! The Russians took me for a whore. I might look like one, and I'm no virgin, but I've never taken money. Isn't that the definition of a whore? I would if I had to; but then I've never lacked money, so I shouldn't boast of my virtue."

"You have known many men."

"Too many."

"Is there a Mr. Davies?"

"That is my maiden name."

"You were married?"

"To a Frenchman."

"You will understand my natural curiosity about your antecedents."

"That is much nicer than 'Who are you?' "

"Our manners improve with practice."

She laughed. "My father was a Welsh adventurer, my mother an English noblewoman. He earned his living by cards and when he was blinded in an accident, he killed my mother and committed suicide. I was sent to a convent in Rouen."

"I once thought of studying there."

"It is much like Dijon though busier because of the river commerce. They are all alike, however, these provincial holes. Well, at fifteen I was seduced by a high ecclesiastic and became his mistress, until he died of apoplexy from over-

eating. Then I married a wealthy importer and we moved to Indochina. Ten years in Saigon and then alcohol did for him, as it will do for me, I fear. I turned down an even dozen proposals, more or less legitimate, took my maiden name, and here I am in the buffet de la gare de Dijon."

"Where do the Penfields come in?"

"Mildred was in the convent. We've kept in touch. I was curious to see if she could still excite me the way she did when we were girls."

"Does she?"

She smiled. "You didn't give me time to find out!"

"Do I excite you?"

She finished her brandy, then said, "Yes, you do."

"Are you in a hurry?"

"No. I like talking with you. There's no hurry."

"What takes you to Cannes?"

"My husband left me a villa at Antibes. I want to see whether to keep it or sell it."

"Then you are not a spy."

"You are sweet, Jack Burgoyne. Have you forgiven me?"

"For what?"

"The rude things I said."

"That was yesterday."

"Is today tomorrow?"

"It grows late. Are you tired?"

"I am not sure. Perhaps in a state of ecstatic fatigue."

"We need fresh air. Which is your hotel?"

"La Bourgogne."

"It belongs to me. I own the entire duchy of Burgundy. It was my grand-patrimony."

"May I be your first duchess?"

"Joyce the Red, all hail!"

She laughed. "I don't know which has gone most to my head—you, the brandy or the trains, but I have never been so happy. Do you learn this art at school?"

"It is the Burgundian bedside manner."

"It's your not wanting anything from me."

"Don't I?"

"Do you?"

"Your hair."

"It's not removable."

"I want to bury my face in it."

"Did you say we needed fresh air?"

"You don't want to see the other trains?"

"Not tonight." She smiled, then said, "I was wrong. I *am* in a hurry."

We went out into the damp air and walked arm in arm up the street. A group of soldiers came toward us, walking in the middle of the street, clinging together and singing drunkenly. We stopped and watched them reel past. They paid no attention to us.

"You haven't told me," she said, "that I smoke and drink too much."

"Do you?"

"Yes."

"Then that's settled."

We reached her hotel on the Place Darcy. The lobby was deserted, the room clerk snoring. We leaned against the wall at the elevator.

"Journey's end," she said, and drew my face to her hair.

We stood for a long moment. Then she opened the elevator door and held it for me.

"Will you?" she asked.

"Willingly," I replied.

We mounted to her room on the fifth and top floor. She undressed swiftly and lay on the bed and waited for me to join her.

It was nearly noon when I awoke. Joyce was still asleep, her hair like fire on the pillow. We had enjoyed long, deliberate and deeply satisfying intercourse, and I felt refreshed. I dressed quietly, and as I was about to leave without waking her, I saw her eyes open. I sat on the edge of the bed. She reached up her arms. I held her and kissed her. She laughed and fell back. On her milk white skin, her body hair was all the redder.

"I had forgotten," she said, "how good it can be."

"You'd think we'd done it for years."

"I wanted you the moment I saw you."

"You nearly drove me away."

"Horrible thought."

"I'm late. Will you be here after lab?"

"I was going to take the seven-thirty *rapide*."

"Don't."

"You want me to stay?"

"Yes."

"What will we do?"

"What we did."

"You want more?"

"Yes."

"So do I. Is there a quiet café where I can sit and have a drink until you come?"

"The Concorde, directly across the Place."

"It will take me until then to get the tangles out of my hair."

"Don't bother. I'll only put them back in."

When I returned at six, I found Joyce seated on the leather *banc* at the Concorde, a Pernod in front of her, a cigarette in her hand. Before she saw me, her face was expressionless as it was when we first met; and then as I approached, her eyes widened, her face relaxed, the lines disappeared and she smiled. We shook hands and I sat beside her and ordered a *demi* of Vézelise, the blonde Pilsner-type beer featured at the Concorde.

"À toi." She lifted her glass and drank it half down, then lit her cigarette and we were enveloped in a cloud of the acrid smoke.

"How is it," I asked, "that you smoke the workers' cigarette?"

"Did we not labor? The truth is, I like everything strong. You!"

"You are a strange one."

"Do you like me?"

"I haven't had time to think about it."

"Did it go well for you? Not too tired?"

"Recharged."

"I too."

"You are not leaving."

"You want me to stay?"

"You are good medicine."

Time passed as we drifted along in quiet talk, she on Pernod, I on beer, there in the peacefulness of the Café de la Concorde, its panelled, gilt-mirrored walls reflecting the older Dijonnais who frequented it as a club. Merchants and professional men and matrons, too, came for apéritifs and tea, chess, the newspapers, and talk. The waiters were old professionals, deliberate, impersonal and skilled. When ours brought more drinks, Joyce's face would resume her habitual green-eyed mask; then when he had left, she turned to me and smiled, her eyes widened and were again amber-flecked.

Toward eight she paid for the accumulation of saucers and we strolled up the Rue de la Liberté to the Place d'Armes and there at a table behind a hedge of potted privet on the *terrasse* of the Restaurant du Pré aux Clercs, we dined on steak, potatoes, salad, and Beaujolais en carafe. It was beginning to grow dark and the pigeons were settling to roost on the ledges of the Hôtel de Ville, the great structure of honey-colored limestone which stood where the Dukes of Burgundy had once built their palace. The vanished rulers were symbolized by stone helmets which rose from the cornices in silhouette against the eggshell sky. A trolley car rocked crazily across the Place and disappeared down the main street with a squeal of flanged wheels.

Our waiter lit the candles on our table, and as we emptied the second carafe, Joyce took my hand across the cloth.

"Mœurs de province," she said. "Bearable only when one knows they are not permanent, that one can escape them."

"But not tonight."

"Not tonight."

I held her knee between my knees; our hands too were joined.

"When?" I asked.

"Let us live each day."

"And night."

"Again so soon?"

"It was long ago."

"We met only yesterday."

"A century ago."

"You are unusually romantic for one studying the sciences."

"You have heard of Arthur Schnitzler? Of Somerset Maugham? Of James Joyce?"

"I have small culture and large appetite."

"I will teach you."

"You have."

We strolled back up the street to her hotel. It was now dark and the bright shop windows offered beautiful displays of mustard jars, gingerbread, and confections, Dijon's specialties on view for the passerby. A soft spring rain was falling as we turned in and again mounted to her room. There we opened the tall windows that looked across a courtyard with elms and chestnuts in leaf to the cathedral of St. Bénigne. The air smelled strong of wet earth, sandalwood and tobacco. Our lips tasted of wine as we stood at the open window in a searching kiss, hearing the sound of rain on the leaves.

And thus a week went by, each day and night the same for us. We met at the Concorde, dined at the Pré aux Clercs, walked up the street to her hotel, stood at the open window and kissed, undressed and made love. Each morning I went away refreshed to the day's work at the Faculty. There were no variations in the slow and muted music that we made. I was not in love as I had known it before, nor even infatuated. When we met in the afternoon, it was as friends, and it was not until we had finished dinner and were holding hands across the table, our knees gripped together, relaxed, assured; and I saw her peaceful, smiling face, that I began to feel desire again.

"Shall we go now?"

"It's lovely not being in a hurry."

"I am now."

"So am I. Go and I will follow."

The Penfields called us a stuffy old married couple. Our sole concession to sociability was to go with them one evening to the movie—René Clair's *Sous les Toits de Paris*.

"Those train whistles," Joyce said, as we talked after love.

"They'll haunt me forever."

"He used them as a leit-motif."

"They'll be ours. That first night at the station! Those Englishmen! I've never known enchantment like this."

"Listen, you can hear the yard engines."

"And the rain on the leaves. Oh Jack, it's too good to last."

I kissed her words away.

Sunday afternoon we walked to the park on the only fine day since she had come. It was the first time I had been there since the winter walk with Erda. Now the trees made a green sky overhead. Thrushes sang. A cuckoo called. Children rolled hoops down the smooth walks. We reached the riverbank and sat on the stone bench. Across the stream the grassy field was the nesting place of larks and they rose up singing.

"I was reading Henry James's *Little Tour in France*," I said, "and it's here on this very bench that he brings it to a close. He did not like Dijon."

"He was probably alone. I'd go mad if I were here alone. I'll remember it because of you."

"You sound sad."

"Nostalgic, I guess, remembering Sunday afternoon walks along the river in Rouen. Now I'll add Dijon to memory."

"What are you telling me?"

"That I'll be leaving."

"No."

"You didn't think I'd stay forever."

"But it's only been a week."

"I intended to stay only a day."

"We could pool our money and share an apartment."

"Money's not the problem."

"What is?"

"You. You are losing weight. You can't go on with such a regime. What you have been lavishing on me belongs to your work."

"I have enough for both. I have never felt better."

"Nothing in excess, my husband used to say when I began on the second bottle of Pernod."

"I've never known one like you. You do not keep me aroused."

71

"I take that as a compliment."

"Stay. We'll find an apartment tomorrow."

"Now you're being that aggressive American. Don't forget, I've loved you because you weren't one."

"Be reasonable."

"I am. Oh Jack, you've been the first who's not sought to reform me. I truly have bad habits and a worse character."

"We have had other things to do."

"Lovely things, and all lovely things do pass. You're poet enough to know that."

"I refuse to be categorized."

She stood up.

"Let's walk. Talking is not good for this afternoon."

She had her way. We wandered back through the park, then returned to town along the riverbank and the canal path, past the hospital and the Faculty and the workers' quarter in the Rue Monge and the statue of Bossuet preaching, a fat pigeon on his head. I showed her a secret garden behind the stone wall of a deserted hotel. There against the side of the building was a well-shrine, with a stone cupid and the inscription "Tout par amor, 1539." Lilacs had grown wild, the bushes were covered with purple blossoms, the air sweet with their fragrance.

"I could have loved you well," she said. "Why was it not you who came over the convent wall?"

We reached the Place Émile Zola as the fanfare of the P.L.M. began its Sunday afternoon concert—a dozen middle-aged railway workers in sloppy blue and red uniforms, blowing blasts of strident music. We found a table on the *terrasse* of the tiny Café du Midi. The leafy square was thronged with promenading Dijonnais. Children had scrambled atop the iron *pissoir* and were gaping over the crowd at the sweating musicians. We drank warm beer from green bottles. It was a spectacle Breughel would have relished. The music and shouting, barking dogs and roaring motorcycles made conversation impossible.

When it grew dark we walked on to the Pré aux Clercs for dinner. The Place d'Armes was also peopled with promenaders,

the quieter bourgeoisie, and behind the hedge we were able to talk again.

"It's a poem by Rimbaud," I said. "Listen!"

Les tilleuls sentent bon dans les bons soirs de juin.
L'air est parfois si doux qu'on ferme la paupière.

"Where was he when he wrote that?"

"Charleville."

"The dreary north. What escapists you poets are! If I shut my eyes, I'm back in Rouen. Oh Jack, why did it have to be the way it was?"

"Stay and we'll make it over."

"An old drunkard like me? Besides, you're my last man. I intend to live with women after this. Anyway, I'll be dead of lung cancer before I'm forty. Look at my fingers. You'd think I was Chinese. What could I give you? A child? No. The good father took care of that. He told me it was an appendectomy when he destroyed my ability to bear a child. My best gift to you would be my body in alcohol."

"Don't talk like that. You never have before."

"You're hearing the true me. I've hidden her for a week, thanks to you. Now you must face her, you fool."

"Please be reasonable."

"A lovely week for me. I've gained the weight you've lost. The lines are gone from my face. My hair is glossy again."

"Green eyes turned amber."

"You haven't asked anything of me. For God's sake, don't start now."

"Only that you stay for a while."

"You are a damn fool, John Burgoyne."

She began to laugh hysterically and I realized that for the first time she was drunk. I went across the square to the carriage stand, came back for her and we drove to the hotel. There she was quiet, and when we were in bed, she was violent in love, and then lay exhausted. It was nearing eleven when she pushed me gently out of bed.

"Go," she said. "Let us both get a good sleep."

She watched me dress, and then when I was putting on my

shoes, she knelt naked and tied the laces. I buried my face in her hair, as she hugged my knees. Sandalwood, tobacco, wine, and woman were blended in one strong perfume. I drew her up and held her against me.

"You will stay?"

"Yes, but go now. I'm so tired."

"Tomorrow?"

"Oui, à demain. Va t'en, mon amour. Laisse-moi dormir."

She pushed me into the hall and I heard the door lock.

All the next day I was impatient to see her. It was the first time I had not been able to concentrate on my work. On my way to the Concorde I bought a nosegay of lilies of the valley—porte bonheur—the first time I had taken her flowers.

She was not in the café. I crossed the Place to the hotel. The room clerk stared when I asked him to ring Madame Davies.

"She has left."

"What?"

"She is no longer here."

"Do you mean that she has checked out?"

"That is the fact."

"Since when?"

"She left last night, soon after you did."

"Where has she gone?"

"She said that she was taking the de luxe at midnight."

"The Blue Train?"

"That's the one. For the Côte d'Azur. Some people have all the luck. They say it is fine weather down there."

"Doubtless. But did not Madame leave a message for me?"

"She left nothing at all, save the scent of a strange perfume."

"She was alone?"

"But certainly."

I thrust the lilies into my pocket and left the hotel. It had begun to rain. I crossed the square to the Concorde and sat down on the *banc*. The old flat-footed garçon came for my order.

"Monsieur desires?"

"The usual."

"Shall I bring Madame's?"

"She will not be here."

The waiter peered at me, then elaborately wiped off the marble-topped table with his towel.

"Then you are alone," he concluded.

"That, alas, is the exact truth. She took the Blue Train last night."

"I am truly sorry to hear that. You made a brave couple."

"That's life, my friend."

"True. One learns from experience that it is not all roses."

IV

Madeleine

The rainy spring merged into a rainy summer. The vintage failed. A cold wind blew from the east. The natives groaned.

I never heard from Joyce. The Penfields reported that she had sold the villa in Antibes and gone they knew not where.

I finished my studies and received my degree in early autumn. As my two-year fellowship had ended, I prepared to return to the United States and seek a laboratory appointment in or near San Francisco. Then one afternoon I received a letter from a legal firm in San Diego, transmitting a draft for $2,000, drawn on the Dijon branch of the Société Générale. It was the residue of my mother's estate, the very last of her gifts to me; and it decided me to stay on in Europe until it was gone. From all accounts, prospects of employment even for trained scientists were bleak. The Depression was becoming worldwide.

I hoped to write a book for which I had long been reading and making notes, a book on tuberculosis and art, studied in the works of Keats, Stevenson, Katherine Mansfield, and D. H. Lawrence. The latter two had died in France, and the first step would be to go to the south of France where Lawrence had lived his last days and to Italy where he had written *Lady Chatterley's Lover.* There I planned to interview doctors who had treated him and to soak up local color.

I was starved for sun. The golden limestone of the ducal city had lost its glow and gone gray. Dijon had become a morgue of grim weather. And so I closed my small affairs, said my good-byes, and on my last afternoon I called a taxi, stowed my bags therein, and drove to the bank on the Place du Théâtre. There I cashed the draft and took the fifty crisp new thousand-franc notes, folded and buttoned them down in an inner pocket of my coat. They gave me a feeling of great wealth.

Next, I directed the driver to the station, where I checked my baggage through to Nice on the seven-thirty *rapide.* Then I walked back the length of the main street to the Café de

Paris, where I had first seen Erda pass and had met Joyce, said good-bye to the frog-faced proprietor and the waiters, and had a *porto sec* on the house. Then I paid homage to the bronze statue of Jean-Philippe Rameau, and in the courtyard of the Hotel de Ville to that of Claus Slüter, the Flemish sculptor, *imagier aux ducs*, standing aproned in the rain, his mallet and chisel upraised. I thought of them as friends.

Finally I climbed the circular staircase of the stone tower to the lookout platform for a last view over the town. In vain. Rain mist hid all but the nearest buildings, their multicolored tile roofs shining wet, their myriad chimney pots asmoke. Almost directly below v.as the Place d'Armes and the Pré aux Clercs where Joyce and I had dined every night for a week, its *terrasse* deserted, tables and chairs taken in for the winter.

Back on the main street I retraced my steps to the Place Darcy and entered the Concorde for a last *demi* of Vézelise. The old garçon approached, towel on arm.

"Monsieur desires?"

"The same." And when he returned with deliberate tread, carefully wiped the foaming glass and set it on the cardboard coaster, I declared, "You have worked here a long time."

"It will soon be thirty-seven years."

"I leave now. This is my last drink with you."

"I read in the *Progrès* that you completed your studies with honor."

"I have been fortunate here. It was a milieu that suited my temperament."

"It astonishes me that you endured our weather."

"It does not improve."

"It has become absolutely vicious. No spring, no summer, no vintage, and now the Gastronomic Fair is threatened. Soon we shall be entering the Ark."

"They say one enjoys fair weather on the Côte d'Azur. I leave for Nice on the seven-thirty."

"If this proves to be true, I beg of you to dispatch us some of their weather." He drew closer and lowered his voice, employing the subjunctive. "If it should not be indiscreet of me to ask, would you be rendezvousing with Madame?"

79

"You remember her?"

A slow smile spread over his moon face. "But certainly! She did not walk as an ordinary woman walks, but rather with a serpentine motion."

"That is well put, my friend. She was unusually supple."

He looked thoughtful. "You were fortunate in her company."

"I do not forget her, although let me say in all frankness, hers is not a troubling memory."

"It is curious, but I could never identify the perfume she wore."

"It was sandalwood. Her garments were permeated with it from having been hung in closets made of that wood."

"That is extraordinary. Certainly not here in France."

"In Indochina. In Saigon, to be exact."

"What you tell me is truly exotic. Does one enjoy such encounters in your country?"

"Hardly."

"I sometimes fancy that her fragrance lingers here where she sat with you so often."

"You are truly a man of sensitive perceptions."

"It is my métier. One learns from observing people."

I paid. We shook hands.

I went on to the station and dined in the buffet on steak, potatoes, salad, and a *demi-carafe* of Beaujolais. My sense of well-being was boundless.

The *rapide* was on time, its carriages shining from the rain, the couplings billowing steam. I boarded and found an unoccupied first-class compartment. Rain was falling as we left the shelter of the station, and I saw only a blur of lights through the streaming window. I pulled the shade, switched on the blue light, removed my shoes and coat and stretched out on the long seat with my overcoat for blanket. Soon I heard the wheels going over the switch-points at the Swiss junction and I knew we were on the main line south, via the Rhone Valley and Lyon, to the Côte d'Azur.

It was a smooth ride and I slept through the night. When I awoke we were somewhere east of Marseilles, running fast

through low hills forested with pine and oak and a heather-like scrub, yielding to terraced olive orchards. The day was clear, and I knew the weather was warm by sight of the peasants in the fields, stripped to the waist. From Cannes to Nice the train followed the shore. I saw white sails on the water and the colored stucco villas. It was the Blue Coast at last.

My destination was the fishing village of Cros de Cagnes, eight miles west of Nice, where the *pension* called Le Soleil had been recommended by my professor of endocrinology as an unfashionable place of simple comfort and good food. The proprietor, Monsieur Torquet, met me at Nice with an old Citroën carryall. We loaded my bags, he picked up foodstuffs at the wholesale market, and we headed for home.

"As one of our dear friend's students," the proprietor said, "I shall ask you to look at my mother. A sad case, just home from hospital in Nice with what is declared to be a terminal case of cancer."

"I am not a medical doctor."

"Nevertheless, I should value your opinion as to the probability of her surviving through the year."

"I am at your service."

The Soleil stood on the beach, a few hundred yards west of the post office, café, general store, and huddle of fishermen's houses that constituted the village. It was a three-story, faded yellow stucco building with a pink tile roof. I was given a front room on the top floor, overlooking the pebbled beach and the sea and along the coast in each direction. The few guests were French. The English tended to resort in Cannes or Nice; the Americans preferred old Cagnes on the hill in back of the beach.

The Torquet family of several generations staffed the *pension*, and I was asked by the proprietor to look at the old grandmother even before I had unpacked my bags. The entire family gathered around while I stood by her bed. She was stupified with morphine. Her heart was strong, her handclasp powerful. She would probably live thus until the malignant growth on the neck closed her windpipe.

"There is no hope at all, they told us at the hospital," the son whispered.

I nodded in agreement.

"Her room has a view of the maritime Alps," he said. "Mama enjoyed it more than that of the sea. Now she is indifferent, but we leave her here. I must apologize for the smell. Bandaging the dying flesh seems to do no good."

"It is only natural," I said, "when one approaches the end from such a malignancy. Keep her free of pain. That is all that remains. Is that not the main line of the P.L.M.?"

"You came along it this morning. There are good walks beyond it, if you care for such."

"I have a hunger for earth under my feet. They have become calloused from the cobbled streets of Dijon."

They gave me a small study in a summer house in the *pension's* garden; and there I spread out books and notes and spent my mornings in bliss. Before lunch I walked along the beach road to the café, and at an outdoor table under a trellised grapevine, I took an apéritif of the local white wine, mild and slightly sour, and nibbled on the plate of olives that was always served. On the beach across the road, the fishermen's women sat mending nets. The sun was warm, the sea blue and without surf or tide. The flora recalled California: bougainvillea and oleander, the trees of orange and lemon, olive, eucalyptus and pepper, mimosa and persimmon.

I led an idyllic life, at peace in body and mind. Evenings were spent in the *pension* parlor, gossiping with family and guests, listening to the radio, or reading *L'Eclaireur de Nice et du Sud-Est*. Several Frenchwomen came and went. They might have been my sisters for all the effect they had on my senses.

The autumn became winter, as at home, without any perceptible change of weather. The *pension* was absurdly cheap. I foresaw no change until early summer when I planned to move on to Florence.

Then one windy afternoon of early spring I was on the beach in front of the *pension*, practicing a boyhood sport recalled since coming to the Cros. The strand was composed

Madeleine

of egg-size, varicolored igneous pebbles brought down from the Alps by the River Var which emptied into the Mediterranean a few miles east of the village. From two strings of rawhide and a leather pocket obtained from the village shoemaker, I fashioned a sling; and standing on the shore I hurled pebbles at targets along the verge or floating in the water. It was an old sport from which I derived pleasure.

On this particular afternoon when I was pegging away at a partly submerged crate, I felt eyes on me. I turned. A woman was watching me, seated out of the wind with her back against a blue dory. I had not seen her when I came out. She was not one of the *pensioners*. She wore a heavy coat and a red scarf around her black hair. She looked more Italian than French. I finally looked away and turned to walk farther on.

"Don't stop," she called, "I beg of you. You throw beautifully, like a young David."

I walked away without answering, resentful at having my sport interrupted. I was wearing old clothes, and from her allusion, I believed she had taken me for a shepherd from the hills. I walked westward along the beach to a grove of umbrella pines called La Pinède which sheltered another *pension;* and there, beyond her sight, I resumed my slinging.

When I came down for dinner that evening, she was there, seated alone at a corner table, eating with a book in one hand. I felt my face turn red. She did not look up, nor did she gaze my way during the meal. After my embarrassment had passed, I observed her closely. She was beautiful, with creamy skin, black hair braided around her head, a long Greek nose, high forehead, full mouth with curving red lips, long lobed ears set with tiny red drops. An actress, I surmised, come for a secluded rest. I remember her voice, free of the coarse accent which characterizes the speech of the south-eastern French. For the first time since Joyce had gone, I felt a quickening of emotion. Or was it merely remembrance of my rudeness on the beach?

She finished eating before I did, and gathering a shawl around her shoulders, she walked to the front door and left without looking my way. She moved with ease and grace, a

small woman with slim legs and little feet, a mature woman of poise and elegance.

Instead of reading the *Éclaireur* and conversing, I walked to the café and enjoyed a cognac. I returned in an hour, hoping that I might find the newcomer with the family and be introduced. She was not there, nor did she return. I kept from asking about her, and finally gave up and went to my room.

I did not see her in the morning or at lunch. Perhaps she had come and gone. I could have asked. I did not. The current that bore me was languid.

I went for a walk after lunch, striking back across the railroad and the highway into the hills, bushed with wild lavender in flower. I broke off a bunch and tied it to my belt like an enormous sachet. Then I worked my way up and back to the low summit of the first range and there I rested, seeing below me the white-walled farmhouses, red-roofed and blue-shuttered, surrounded by vineyards and olive orchards. Brimming cisterns gleamed amid clumps of dark pines. I could hear the chop-chop of hoes, the sounds of children at play and barking dogs, and a man's high voice singing a folk song. Down below from where I had come, the blue sea was molded like a mirror to the shore. In the west I could see the Esterel range beyond Cannes. I stretched out and dozed.

The sun was nearly set when I started home. I passed terraced fields of night-blooming jasmine where peasant women were watering the plants. They would return before sunrise and harvest the flowers for the perfume factories at Grasse.

It was twilight when I reached the railroad back of the village. The northbound Blue Train was due to pass through at five forty-five. I was used to hearing it each evening as I washed up for dinner, flying by with a shriek of its whistle.

Now I leaned on the lowered crossing-gate and waited. In the half-light the tiny station was almost hidden by an enormous purple bougainvillea. Then the rails began to hum. The train was coming. I felt my skin prickle with gooseflesh. The whistle sounded, and suddenly there it was, drawn by the great black engine with copper-banded boiler gleaming in the fading light. Like a mad angel the train swept by, the blue and

yellow *wagons-lit* with lighted windows and blurred faces. The red lights of the *fourgon* glared back, then vanished around the curve of track. I heard the whistle, wailing for the next village, and the diminishing sound of rolling wheels on iron rails. There remained a light pall and smell of coal smoke. And silence. My heart was pounding.

The old crossing guard hobbled out to raise the barrier. He saw me still leaning on it, and muttered a *bon soir.*

"It really rolls," I said, with a gesture down track.

"I should think so," he croaked. "It's making eighty when it passes here. They say it makes a hundred before it reaches Cannes." He tugged on the wheel and the barrier slowly rose. "They eat well, I'm told, and they sleep together. What follies those passengers enjoy!" He rubbed his hands together, chuckled, and crept back in to his meal.

It was that evening after dinner that I met her. Her name was Mademoiselle Montrechet. We remained in the family group at first, and then as they settled into their routines of cards and sewing, she and I withdrew to a wicker settee in a corner of the parlor.

"You are not still annoyed with me?" she asked.

"Was I ever?"

"Yesterday when I drove the young David from his favorite place."

"I believed you took me for a yokel. I regret the rudeness I displayed."

"It was I who was forward."

"Did you know I was a *pensioner?*"

"Of course. The little hunchback slavey pointed you out to me before I went to the shore."

"Emma is a beastly gossip. I have had to forbid her to interrupt my work."

"I would not have taken you for an American."

"They say my French blood shows."

"Only an American, however, would think of making sport with a sling. It impressed me as infinitely droll."

"I am not used to performing for an audience." I paused. "Nor such a beautiful one."

"Are all Americans such flatterers?"

"I do not see people in nationalistic terms. I see them first as human beings. I see you first as a woman. But I confess, I do not know your nationality, and I am curious."

"Let me test your cleverness."

"Are you Italian?"

"It is true that I am often taken for such because of my features and complexion. Actually, I am French. My mother is of Pau in the Basses-Pyrenées, my father Parisian, a professor of history. I was born in Paris, but I often go to Pau and its environs."

"Then you must have Basque blood or Spanish."

"I myself have never been beyond the borders of France."

"Do you know Burgundy?"

"Only the Morvan. My father directed researches there in pre-Roman Gaul. I used to go with him when I was little. There are many Celtic traditions to be found there, as well as menhirs and dolmens."

"And Vézelay?"

"Very well. A most beautiful sanctuary."

"If I may ask without being indiscreet, are you an actress?"

"Heavens no! Why would you think that?"

"Because of your beauty and your way of carrying yourself. Do not think me forward if I say that I felt an urge last evening to rise and follow you out."

She laughed. "Do you flatter all women this way? I must consult Emma."

"I have been a recluse for months. Tell me though, are you not connected with the arts?"

"Are all Americans as curious as you, or is it something you learned in your studies?"

"My interest *is* in research."

"And you regard me as raw material!"

"Don't say that. But you are a wonderful specimen."

"I assure you of the regularity of my natural functions."

"I have already taken your pulse."

"Without holding my wrist?"

"From the artery that throbs in your neck."

"Is it poetry that you write in the summerhouse?"

"No, but I am a devoté of the Symbolists. Myself, I am writing another kind of work."

"Do you ever read it aloud? My English needs practice."

"I might be persuaded." I paused. "You are the first woman I have talked with in a long time."

"I am honored."

"I do not mean it that way."

"What do you mean?"

"I feel drawn to you by instinct. Do not misunderstand me. I have no carnal motive."

She laughed. "You are a man. All men are carnal. Therefore . . ."

"Do not tease me."

"I do not tease you, my friend, but you say and do things that afford me vast amusement."

"Have you been here before?"

"Each year on holiday."

"You work then."

"Yes, I work."

"May I ask at what?"

"You are also a persistent man. I will tell you. I am a journalist. I am on the staff of *L'Œuvre*."

"I used to read it occasionally, but not since I have been here. *L'Éclaireur* is the local bible."

"I read no papers when I am on holiday."

"You live in Paris."

"Do you like my city?"

"Not in December. I am a southerner. I will visit you in Pau. I have never seen your Southwest."

"Why did you come to France?"

"Primarily to engage in endocrinological research. I had a fellowship."

"Then you are a doctor of medicine?"

"Of science. I was a medical student at home but gave it up to come to France."

"Why did you discontinue that line of study?"

"It was my father's wish that I follow him as an M.D. He

died when I was in my teens. I sought to carry out his wish, and until my mother died two years ago, I did so, successfully—and unhappily. Her death left me free, and also with a small income. I determined to study pure science in the land of my ancestors."

"They say physicians are badly needed in your country."

"I am lacking in social conscience."

"You are an individual. That is what brought you home to France."

"I had tired of the group life we led as students. Here in France one is left alone."

"That is indeed our character."

"I thrived in Dijon, but once my degree was granted and I received a small inheritance, I came to this milder climate."

"Jean de Bourgogne is now Jean de la Côte d'Azur. Do you practice any of the arts?"

"I paint."

"Here?"

"Once in the refectory at the Faculty."

"An odd place for such."

"We painted the goddess of love under diagnosis by the class. All of us were involved in a kind of Burgundian Rembrandt."

"What was your part in it?"

"I painted a wart on her rump."

She laughed. "How very droll you are!" She looked at her wrist watch. "It grows late. I must go. We have talked at such length!"

"I ended up talking instead of asking."

"I must say good-night to my sister."

"Is she here with you?"

"She is with friends at La Pinède."

"May I accompany you?"

"Please, no."

She left again by the front door.

Although I saw her after dinner on succeeding nights, she was reserved. Had I been too bold? Had my eyes showed the hunger she stimulated in me? Though I was attracted by her, I

Madeleine

also sensed that she did not welcome ardent attention. Each evening after we had talked awhile, she excused herself to say good-night to her sister. I managed to restrain my curiosity and cool my ardor.

Then one evening she went to her room after dinner and returned with a book. It was *Lady Chatterley's Lover*, in English.

"I bought it in Nice today," she said. "My friends in Paris have been talking about it. Will you help me over some of the difficult parts? My English is so slight."

"Do you know how naughty it is?" I teased.

"How so? The subject is love, is it not? Is that regarded as naughty in your country?"

"That depends on who does the loving."

"Just so."

She read aloud where we sat in the corner, haltingly with a thick accent, I helping her to pronounce and to translate. The parlor thinned out until at last we were alone. It was the first night she had not gone to La Pinède. At ten-fifteen we put down the book and heard the B.B.C. news from London.

"This Mellors," she said when the broadcast was over, "he is not like any Frenchman I have known. Do you as an American understand his psychology?"

"I don't know what you mean 'as an American.' As a man, yes, I do. His wanting to remain aloof. I have felt that way. I do feel that way. Or do I?" My eyes sought hers. She turned her face. They she spoke again.

"A strange thing, this love out-of-doors. Lawrence seemed to have a passion for it."

"We love nature more than you do. I wish you would come with me for a walk in the hills. They are so beautiful now with the lavender in bloom. I am going again to Vence where Lawrence is buried to visit the sanitarium where he died. I need to copy his chart to use in my book. Go with me, I beg of you."

"I must be with my sister."

"Is she ill?"

"I can only say that she needs me."

She rose. I saw that she was troubled. She said good-night and went to her room.

I was puzzled. My life was so well ordered that I was reluctant to become involved, and apparently she felt the same. And yet we were mutually attracted.

I made the pilgrimage to Vence, found Lawrence's grave, and met the physician who had attended him in his last illness. He allowed me to copy the chart. There had not been an autopsy.

Back on the beach at day's end, triumphant at the success of my quest, I broke a spray of bloom from the mimosa tree in front of the *pension.* The pollen-heavy fragrance excited me. I wanted her to smell it. She was at table when I came in. My heart pounded. I gave her the little branch. She smelled it, then looked at me curiously.

"From his grave?"

"From the tree of life. It is for you. Breathe its fragrance. Drink one of the golden balls in your wine. You will live forever."

"What makes you so fantastic this evening?" Her eyes widened.

"You do." Her eyes dropped. "May we talk later?" I dreaded her reply. She looked up.

"Yes," she said. "I'd like that."

Our eyes held for a long moment. Then I went to wash up. I stared in the mirror. The current had quickened.

We sat later on the settee while the parlor hummed around us. I was tongue-tied for the first time, afraid to speak lest I reveal my desire. Again she read from *Lady Chatterly* and we talked about Lawrence and my day.

Then the B.B.C. came on. "This is London," the distant voice spoke. We were alone. The others had retired, not caring for news in English.

Then for the first time I felt the heat of her leg next to mine. She must have sensed my awareness, for her body suddenly changed. What circuit had been joined? Had the mimosa proved a love charm? Or could it be Lawrence's ghost, drawn by her voice? Whatever it was, I knew that we

had come together after touch and go; and in that moment of revelation, I sought to control my trembling body, while the calm voice recounted the world's woe. My hand sought hers and closed over it. Now it was she who trembled. The news ended. The Mayfair Hotel dance band came on, playing "Penthouse Serenade."

I stood and held out my hand. She rose and I took her in my arms, and we moved slowly over the blue and white linoleum floor among the empty tables and chairs. I held my body away from hers. Only my hand, resting lightly on the small of her back, felt the warmth of her flesh, and my cheek next to her hair knew its softness. I breathed her fragrance, a perfume faint and delicate. The music quickened into "Sailing on the Robert E. Lee," and round and round we moved in tempo.

When it ended, she disengaged herself and went out the front door. Was she bound for La Pinède? I waited a moment, then followed. She was leaning against the trunk of the mimosa tree, the tree of life. The charm, the charm! A full moon cast a glittering track over the water. Her body was arched against the tree, her face uplifted to the moon like a priestess. The air was redolent with mingled scent of mimosa, eucalyptus, rose-geranium, and sea wrack. The only sound was of the little waves of the tideless sea, breaking softly on the shingle. The night was enchanted. I stood close, so that our knees touched.

"Aren't we getting behind in our reading?" she asked, matter of fact.

The spell was broken. She had run outdoors to break it. I leaned away.

"We are like Paolo and Francesca," I said. "Dante tells how they were reading together in the garden, and when they came to a certain passage, they turned and kissed and read no more that day."

"How persuasive you Americans are!"

"I am only a man."

"How persuasive you men are! But my arms are cold. I go in."

I followed. She was not in the parlor. I went upstairs. Her

91

room was also on the top floor at the back of the *pension*, overlooking the mountains. A light shone from under her door. I knocked. She opened it.

"Madeleine," I pleaded. It was the first time I had used her name. "Madeleine, dear one, don't run away. Come to my room. There is a marvelous passage in Lawrence I want to read to you. Not in *Lady Chatterley*. It is in another of his books, one that I bought in Nice. Come and hear."

She allowed me to lead her by the hand, and we tiptoed down the dark hall. We heard footsteps below, and then a door shut softly. We stood listening. In a moment the stink of death drifted up to us. The son had given his mother her eleven o'clock injection. Madeleine shuddered and clung to me. I led her into my room and locked the door.

She stood by the lukewarm radiator. All I could offer in the way of refreshment was an apple. She bit into it, then handed it to me to bite. In a moment I read from *Apocalypse:*

What man most passionately wants is his living wholeness and living unison, not his own isolate salvation of his 'soul.' Man wants his physical fulfilment first and foremost, since now, once and once only, he is in the flesh and potent. For man, the vast marvel is to be alive. Whatever the unborn and the dead may know, they cannot know the beauty, the marvel of being alive in the flesh. We ought to dance with rapture that we should be alive in the flesh, and part of the living incarnate cosmos.

"That is beautiful the way you read it," she said, when I put the book down. "I am not sure I understand it all, but I won't ask you now to make a translation."

"You see it was not a deception. I *did* want to read to you."

I took the apple core from her and put it on the table. Then I stood facing her. She looked at me quizzically, as if to ask, how came we here? She was so beautiful that I could not keep from reaching out my hand and caressing her bare arm. Her eyes spoke to me. My arm went around her waist. I found her eager to be kissed.

We leaned against the radiator in that first long embrace. But when I grew bold, she gently freed herself, unlocked the door and slipped away. I followed and tried her door. It was locked.

I went back to my room, my body alert and glowing. I undressed and stood naked on the balcony. From beyond the village came the coughing roar of an African lion. A little ambulatory circus had arrived that day and pitched its caravan on the shore. I gradually cooled off, then chilled, and went to bed. Sleep came quickly.

I did not see her all the next day. She did not come down for lunch. I knocked on her door afterward. No answer. I tried the knob. Locked. I walked along the beach past La Pinède, as far as the willow-grown mouth of the Cagnes. I did not see her. Had she left? I feared to ask. My mind kept turning over each detail of the night before. What had I done to drive her away? All I could think of was Madeleine Montrechet.

After returning from the walk I sat blankly over my notes in the sunroom. The door opened. It was Emma, the slavey.

"I thought perhaps your basket needed emptying."

"It is as empty as I."

The little hunchback sidled closer. "What troubles you, Monsieur Jean?"

"Have you seen Mademoiselle?"

Her beaked face opened in a gold-toothed grin. "You're lovesick," she cackled.

"Answer me."

"Not since breakfast."

She fingered the edge of the table with a claw hand, then looked up, half sly, half wistful.

"Do you think she is beautiful?" she asked.

"Very."

"And desirable?"

"Utterly."

"And I? I am ugly. Is it not so?"

"Everyone loves you, little witch that you are."

"But no one wants to sleep with me. Only those stinking

fishermen, so drunk they don't know who I am."

I laid my hand on her lank black hair, but she broke away, sobbing, and scuttled out the door.

I walked to the café later and drank a *chopine* of white wine that raised my spirits. When she did not appear for dinner, I despaired again. At eight o'clock there was a broadcast from Prague of the *Bartered Bride*. I pulled my chair close to the loud-speaker and sought solace in Smetana's joyous music.

During the first entr'acte, as I sat with my face bent over in my hands, I heard the front door open. I peered through the bars of my fingers. It was Madeleine, hair wind-blown, cheeks flushed, eyes sparkling. I rose eagerly. She greeted me impersonally and took a hand of cards from one of the family.

Her face told me nothing. She laughed and was gay. I closed my eyes and returned to the music.

Ten o'clock came and still she played cards. Finally she rose and came over to the radio. I stood up.

"Bonne nuit," she said, holding out her hand.

I took it. A note transferred to mine. After she had left the room, I sat down with my back to the parlor, unfolded the note and read it.

"Come to my room, if it pleases you."

I could hardly sit through the London news. At ten-thirty I went to my room, took a sponge-off, donned robe and slippers, and stepped out on my balcony. Again the glitter lay on the water. The fishing fleet was scattered darkly over the bay. I breathed a prayer to Diana and went to Madeleine's room.

She answered my knock in a soft voice. I entered. She sat at the dresser with her back to me, brushing her long hair. Our eyes met in the mirror. Her face was grave. I went to the back of her low bench and stood. Her fragrance dizzied me. I laid my hands on her shoulders. She wore a thin blue silk kimono which did not insulate the heat of her body. She continued to brush her crackling hair.

"You wanted to come?" she asked.

I buried my face in her hair. She laid down the brush.

"Did you look for me today?"

"I thought you had gone."

"I had to go to Nice. I longed for you, my love, dear Jean." It was the first time she had called me that. "I feared you would be angry at my running away last night, like a foolish girl. I had to. I was not well."

She rose, still facing the mirror. "Tonight I am well."

Her kimono opened and and she let it slide to the floor. I saw her body in the glass, the rosy-nippled breasts, the love hair a dense black against the ivory of her skin.

I let my robe fall to the floor, turned her gently to face me, took her in my arms and carried her to the bed.

When finally we lay side by side, she said, "I have never loved an American before. Am I as good as the women of your country?"

"You have had my virginity."

She laughed. "Do you like me?"

"Do you seek another proof?"

"In a moment, but first, let me hear you say it."

"From the very first sight, sitting there out of the wind, black hair, red scarf, blue boat."

"You wondered?"

"No. I was mainly angry with you. But I did that night, when I watched you walk, not even glancing at me. I did not dream, however, that it would be thus."

"Nor did I."

"Are you ready now for the second proof?"

"Oh, but I am! Will you teach me the American ways?"

She turned on her side and drew me to her.

Day was breaking when I went to my room.

I slept until noon. On my way down to lunch I knocked at her door. No answer. It was locked. She was not in the dining room. I worked in the sunroom without the torment of the day before.

At four o'clock I heard the latch click as someone entered the garden gate. I knew that it was Madeleine. The door opened and there she stood, breathing hard, her face troubled. I moved to embrace her but she held me off.

"Oh my dear," she said, "a terrible thing has happened. My sister's friend committed suicide this morning. I can tell you

no more now. I must return immediately."

My heart stopped. "To Paris?"

"To La Pinède, where my sister is. I ran all the way only to tell you where I am and that I cannot see you tonight."

"Can I be of help?"

"Friends have come from Nice. I must return now. Au revoir." She kissed me and left.

I read the story of the tragedy that evening in the *Éclaireur*. It was an affair of Lesbianism. The sister's "friend" was an "amie." Madeleine had come from Paris in an effort to dissuade her younger sister from further relations with an older Frenchwoman, a dilettante who had seduced the girl and brought her to the Riviera. Madeleine had apparently succeeded in persuading her sister to break away and accompany her back to Paris. Whereupon the chagrined Lesbian superficially wounded the girl, then shot herself successively through both heart and temple, a feat which the newspaper termed, "tout à fait miraculeux."

Madeleine did not return to Le Soleil that night nor for breakfast the next morning. As I was walking to the café toward noon, a Renault sedan overtook me. A handkerchief fluttered at the window. It was Madeleine, and a young woman and two men I had never seen before. I feared that she had had to leave without our meeting again. I worked all afternoon in blind concentration.

I went to my room after dinner and read in the only souvenir I had of her—a volume of François Mauriac's poems called *Orages* which she had loaned me. They were bittersweet poems of love won and love lost and of the burden carried by a sensual man. They spoke to me with a voice I had never heard in poetry. I read them now with new intensity and deeper meaning.

At last I turned out the lamp and went on my balcony. There was diminished light from the gibbous moon. No boats were on the water. The lighthouses of Ferrat and Antibes wheeled and stabbed. I ached for Madeleine. Had I lost her?

I lay down on my bed and must have dozed.

I was roused sometime later by a soft knocking on the door.

"Who is it?"

"C'est moi, Madeleine."

It was she, in coat, hat, and veil, beautiful and melting. I held her close and she put her cheek against mine.

"I need you, my love, Oh how I need you!" she murmured.

"You have me."

"I feared you would not be here. Your window was dark and there was no light under your door."

"I thought it was good-bye you waved this noon."

"So much has happened. You read in the paper, yes? You know then. It is ended. I put her on the Blue Train before they could detain her for an inquest, then I came to you as soon as I was able, my American lover."

"Who were those men in the car?"

"Only my cousins from Nice. You were jealous?"

"I have had gloomy thoughts. Now you have turned them golden."

"Don't put on the light. I must look like a witch. Let me go and bathe. Will you come then? The night is yours."

It was a beautiful night. Madeleine had seen the body of the dead Lesbian—the first corpse she had ever viewed—and in response to her sister's wish had helped wash and dress it for burial. The effect had been to turn her back toward life, so that I found her needful of my living body, her desire heightened to an almost unbearable ecstasy. We strove with all our might to perpetuate the life in us.

I awoke at daybreak and again slipped away to my own bed.

She rested in her room for the next twenty-four hours, then on the morning of the second day we went on an outing. I had read in the *Éclaireur* that the Italian liner "Rex," Genoa for New York, was due to call at Villefranche for passengers. We planned to be there when she put into the bay. They packed a lunch for us, and we set out by autobus to Nice, where we transferred to the Mentone bus.

Villefranche clings to the ankle of the Grande Corniche, a few miles east of Nice, its tall stucco houses forming a pastel conglomeration against the gray cliffs, two shades of green

being supplied by terraced stands of olive and pine. The long finger of bay points seaward, bounded on each side by a narrow wooded cape.

We left the bus where the highway crosses the neck of the western cape, then followed a dirt road through pines on the crest until we had nearly reached the end of the cape. There we turned off and found a vantage point on the steep eastern slope. The blue bay was below us, its water unruffled under a windless sky. We were in a clearing among the pines, the ground carpeted with dead needles, the air fragrant with resin. I twitched a branch and a shower of pollen sifted down like yellow dust.

Madeleine lay on her back on the bed of needles. She wore a slack suit of fine-ribbed green corduroy, espadrilles on her bare feet. It was the first time I had seen her in casual clothes. I leaned on my elbow and watched the small boats coming in and out of the narrow bay.

"I brought your book," I said, reaching in my shirt and removing the little volume. "Do you know Mauriac? I mean, know him personally?"

"I do. He is a man of great feeling and kindness. He has been very good to me with the tenderness that comes to a few older men who have lived deeply sensual lives."

"His poetry expresses much suffering."

"It is from the struggle between soul and senses. It is obvious that he is an ardent Catholic. I trust you did not overlook the book's motto: *les derniers grondements d'une jeunesse que s'éloigne*. How does one say that in English?"

"One doesn't, at least not literally. I believe I know what it means."

"So do I! Oh Jean, my friend, it is more and more meaningful as my own youth recedes."

"Dare I ask your age, O ageless one?"

She laughed. "You express yourself so nicely. I really believe you should remain in France and enrich our culture."

"You tease me."

"Indeed I do not. I am a serious woman."

"Of what age?"

"You have been persistent almost from the first when, you will recall, you rejected my overture. But why do you need to ask my age, you who can take a woman's pulse without even touching her?"

"Thirty?"

"Oh thank you, you are truly a friend, but alas, you must add six."

"Such antiquity! All of eight years my senior. Soon we'll *both* be in our thirties."

"You will age well. You have learned good things."

"The most from you, my Madeleine."

At eleven o'clock, precisely on schedule, the bow of the "Rex" appeared from behind the eastern cape. She entered the bay and dropped anchor abreast of us, her twin black funnels banded with the Italian colors, a red and white house flag flying from her afterpeak. Steam rose from the fore-funnel, followed by a deep blast that was hurled back by the cliff.

We sat with drawn-up knees and watched a lighter with passengers and baggage approach and disgorge into the ship. Then she backed out of the bay and disappeared behind the western cape.

"Do you wish you were on board?" she asked.

"If you were with me."

"Are you never homesick?"

"Only lovesick."

I kissed her, but after a brief surrender, she freed herself.

"No you don't, Mr. Mellors. Morning in the open air is not a proper place."

"We could go beneath the pines where no eye would see us."

"The needles would hurt my flesh, and besides my ensemble is not fashioned for such an act."

"I am nevertheless very happy."

"You have been in love before."

"Never like this. You are a kind of incarnation of all the women I have ever known."

"You are an incorrigible flatterer. Are you not hungry? I die of hunger, being unaccustomed to such a vigorous life."

We lunched on bread and cheese and meat, and there was a wicker-covered bottle of chianti. The wine made us glow and she let me love her a little and gently, but mostly she wanted to talk.

"Ah, but you're a city girl," I said, bending over her. "The wonder is you are so healthy with no outdoor life at all. Everything about you is perfection: skin, hair, teeth."

"I have never been made love to so clinically. I like it. Tell me though, how long before I fade?"

"Never, if you follow my prescription of the other night. One golden bloom in wine taken with the evening meal. It would be best if I could prepare it for you."

"But you will be returning to your country."

"Not until summer. Come with me to Italy, to the villa near Florence where Lawrence wrote the book. Let us honeymoon there."

"Do not torment me, I beg of you. It is a miracle that I am here now."

"Where should you be?"

"In Paris, of course. Imagine how difficult it was to send my sister back alone. Our cousins were angry with me. I can tell you now. 'For that beachcomber?' they asked, when I pointed you out as we drove by. I was furious that they saw only the worn clothes and not you. It was then that I decided to stay."

"Did you see more than old clothes that first afternoon?"

"I saw your thin face, your wiry frame, your brown hands, and, oh, the way you selected the small stones and most delicately rubbed them clean before putting them in the sling. The grace of your movements. It was a marine tableau, a poem of utmost charm. I was drawn to you in spite of my wish to remain aloof, and that is why I spoke to you. Only to be ignored. Ah God, I blushed and would not raise my eyes to you that night."

"Why did you wish to remain aloof?"

"I wanted only to free my sister. I did not want a love affair. I am not a green girl, you know, in search of experience."

"Are you married?"

"Do not catechize me."

"Why did you let me love you?"

"I could not help it. I sought to remain impersonal, but in vain. You provoked in me exquisite feelings that I thought myself no longer capable of; and when I perceived that you are an artist, as well as a scientist, and that you know something of the way women are and would not be foolish or clumsy, then I gave myself to you with all my heart."

"But you won't out of doors."

"It would not be successful here."

"You French are more cold-blooded than we are."

"And wiser. You have lived among my people and our blood is in you so that you are not alien to me. You and your ways are a seductive blend of the familiar and the strange. How could I resist you?"

"You will come with me?"

"You must not ask that. It is not fair, for I cannot. I must return to Paris."

"When?"

"Tomorrow."

"Tomorrow?"

"I had not meant to tell you until tonight when you were leaving me. I must take the Blue Train."

"Then this is the last time."

"We have all day, all night."

I lay face down on the prickly needles and sought to hold back tears of chagrin. I felt unable to match her resignation.

"I did not want to love you either," I said finally. "For long I did not touch a woman, even a handclasp, but gave myself utterly to my work. The Cros was like Eden, without Eve."

"It was unnatural for you to remain chaste so long."

"You are so utterly French."

"What else, my love, what else would you have me?"

"I will always be hungry for you. Can we be together in Paris? I shall be there en route from Italy to England."

"When lovers part they can never come together again the same two persons. Time alters them. Time and distance. Who knows what they will do to us? There will be war again. There

is always the fear of the Germans, the modern barbarians. The paper I work for is international in outlook and policy, but in my heart I do not believe. I fear."

"You are too fatalistic."

"Life has taught me to be."

"I have yet to learn."

"You must learn to take all when the time is ripe, as ours was. You must never forget the nature of idylls. They bud, they bloom, they fade."

"You leave even before ours is through blooming."

"That is our fate. I would have you think of this enchanted coast and those who have loved here before us. Phoenicians, Greeks and Romans, the barbarians, Italians, French. And now we two, Jean and Madeleine. Think of us, my love, as two of the brightest links in the long chain."

We dozed, side by side on the pine needles under the blue sky and golden showers of pollen.

Twilight found us back in Nice at the Café Monod on the Place Masséna, where English tea and Sandeman's port engendered more talk.

"There is no point in a man enjoying women," she said, "if he does not learn to apply to the next all that he has learned from the ones before. You did not come to me a gauche shepherd. You brought things learned from those you have told me of, all of them, even Nancy. And do you know the greatest thing a man or a woman can learn?"

"Tell me."

"That it is more satisfying to give pleasure than to receive it. But you do know this. We both do. That is why we are so good together."

"But after tonight you will stop giving."

"Then it is your turn, to give me the freedom to go. What if I had gone day before yesterday, as every reasonable impulse told me to do?"

"I shall never forget your coming to my darkened room."

"It was a supreme moment for me as well."

"Tell me how it is that you are beautiful and not vain or selfish?"

"I was once both."

"What can I hope for in a woman after you?"

"Your new wisdom and strength will attract good women. Like unto like. You must marry and father children."

"You have borne children?"

"Yes."

"That is why you are tender with me."

"Oui, mon enfant."

"One more?"

"Perhaps. It would be truly a love-child."

We walked across the Place to the Cagnes autobus stand, seeing the electric signs on the buildings—Aux Galeries Lafayette de Paris; L'Eté à Aix-les-Bains; Hotel Ruhl et des Anglais; Nestlé, Trésor des Mamans; Ostende, Belgique, Reine des Plages; Voyages en Italie—all the glittering signs, casting their light down on us.

We ate dinner at her table, and in honor of her departure, Monsieur Torquet opened an old bottle of St. Emilion. She was gay and adorable, and I loved her joyfully, hopelessly.

We went at once to her room after we had eaten, and undressed; and not wanting to make love in the dark, we dimmed the lamp with her red scarf. I remember that sometime toward morning she leaned over me and stroked my closed eyelids and whispered, "When you see me no longer, remember how I caressed your face." She lay back down and said, even softer, "Soon I will be old. And you as well, my love. How beautiful life is, how sad!"

I slept again until noon. She left a farewell note under my door. "I shall look for you when the Blue Train passes." There was also a sprig of lavender from a bouquet I had brought her.

Toward evening I leaned once again on the barrier and waited for the Blue Train to pass. It came with a shriek and a rush; and it went, leaving the dying sound of its wheels and the acrid smell of coal smoke. Was it she I saw at the window, waving? I could not be sure, so swift was the passage of the train.

The old man crept out to raise the barrier. This time I did not linger to talk with him.

V

Martha

My life at Le Soleil ended with the departure of Madeleine. I bought an excursion ticket to Italy that allowed stopovers in any city. Florence was the only one where I stayed a while, and there it was to visit the Villa Mirenda at Scandicci in the nearby countryside, where I sought vestiges of Lawrence's residence. From Rome I went to Naples and there obtained passage on a Dutch freighter to Rotterdam. A slow voyage with calls at Marseilles, Barcelona, and Casablanca saw my book finished, and I arrived midsummer in London with free time and a little money left.

I bought a Royal Mail freighter passage to California via Panama Canal three weeks hence, then settled into a Bloomsbury boardinghouse and passed the days in galleries, museums, libraries, and parks, and in the reading room of the Royal College of Physicians, examining the earliest editions of Vesalius and Paré, rare books that were never made available by French libraries to mere students.

The time was early summer, the weather fair, tourists few. The Depression cut deeply into foreign travel. London was sedate after Paris and Rome. It was my first visit to the British capital and I liked it more than I thought I would, responding to the sober English character, the friendliness of the people in the streets, and their sense of self-reliance and certainty.

I sought to understand what Madeleine had given me. I felt mature at last and ready for whatever life held for me. As for loving another woman, I could not conceive of one to match the gifts of the Frenchwoman I had known so briefly and yet with such powerful effect. Besides, the English women were unalluring.

Then one morning at the American Express I found a letter from my cousin Robert, the son of my mother's sister, a coffee and tea importer in San Francisco, which read in part:

"Dear Jack, Mother gave me your travel letter saying you

106

will be in London for a few weeks, and I hasten to ask you to be nice to my fiancée Martha Cameron. She'll be there about the same time as you with her mother on her way back from Munich. I wanted her to get married a year ago, but she insisted on going, and now she's due back and we'll get married in Piedmont. I hope you'll be back for it. Business is very good for us in spite of the Depression—you know how people like their morning drink—and if you wanted to go into business I sure could make you a lot of money in this operation. Enclosed is a twenty for you and her to take in a show or two, and if there's any left over, bring me a Dunhill pipe, the kind with a short straight stem and a medium bowl. Be good to Martha but not too good.

Yours, Bob."

His letter was followed a day later by a note from Martha Cameron, giving her London hotel address. It was another few days before I overcame inertia and wrote, suggesting a rendezvous at the American Express office in the Haymarket; and it was there in the lobby that we met in mutual appraisal.

"So you are Bob's cousin Jack!"

"At your service, Miss Cameron."

"Out of a sense of duty."

"And curiosity."

"How do I look?"

"Cool."

"Do you really like it? I got it in Prague."

She was wearing a coarse linen skirt and a white blouse embroidered with red and blue flowers, and sandals on her bare feet.

"They say it's going to be another hot day. You are sensible to dress this way."

"Where are we going?"

"Lyon's Corner House. Do you mind eating there?"

We walked to the top of the Haymarket to the restaurant around the corner, and there we were seated at a marble-topped table in a quiet corner.

She was not pretty. Her eyes were small and close set, but a clear blue. Her nose was too large for her freckled face, her

hair sand color. Her mouth was her best feature, wide and generous, the lower lip full, almost bee-stung. Her hands, as they played nervously with the silver before we were served chilled salads, toast and tea, were long fingered and blue veined. Her bare arms were white and also freckled. She was as tall as I, with shapely legs and feet. Her breasts swelled the flowered blouse.

"Well," she said. "Do you like what you see?"

"I can't decide whether you're a farm or a chorus girl."

She laughed. "I *was* born in the country, but on a vineyard, not a farm."

"Where did you meet Bob?"

"At Cal."

"I suppose you have been studying German business methods."

"Heavens no."

"What then?"

"Art."

"Art?"

"Why do you look astonished?"

"I can't imagine Bob . . ."

"I know. You think he's a Philistine. He is."

"Why are you marrying him?"

"Aren't you being rather personal, Dr. Burgoyne?"

"How would you like me to be?"

"Yourself."

"All right then, why are you marrying him?"

"He loves me."

"And you don't love him?"

"I didn't say I didn't."

"He and I are not alike."

"What are you like?"

"I like painting. Do you paint?"

"I try."

"Have you been to the Tate?"

"I haven't been anywhere in London. Mother is a hypochondriac. I've been devoting myself to her."

"When is the marriage?"

"This fall. Will you come?"

"If I get an appointment in the Bay region."

"Bob says you're a brain."

"I also have an organ called the heart."

"Tell me about its beat."

"Regular."

"I expected to find you terribly intellectual. You're really quite . . ."

"Ordinary."

"Entertaining is what I was going to say."

"I said I was at your service."

"It's a relief to be with an American man."

"Are Germans on the make?"

"They think art students are to bed down."

"Well?"

"I'm really a Puritan."

"All but your mouth."

"What do you mean?"

"It was made for kissing."

"I promised Bob I'd wait till we were married."

"Haven't you ever?"

"With him, naturally, but not with anyone else."

She put down her fork and took a swallow of tea and leaned forward on her elbows. "The marble feels cool, doesn't it. You're not an M.D., I know, but you have studied and know a lot."

"And lived a bit."

"I need to talk to someone."

"I'm here. What about?"

"Bob."

"Yes?"

"He can never make love to me without drinking a lot first."

"It sounds like he is the Puritan. There are many fetishes some find necessary before they can have intercourse."

"I'd like to think I'm fetish enough."

"I'd say you are."

She laughed. "I confess to loving it, fetish and all."

"The year must have been a long one to go without."

"Long in every way. I've had time to think."

"About marrying Bob?"

"About everything. I'm glad you'll let me unburden."

"Bob's a money-maker. And you'll never be out of tea and coffee."

She laughed again. "I've grown up with money. Dad owns the Beau Soleil winery and lots of other things. This year I've learned other values."

"My grandfather owned a vineyard. I went to see it in Auxerre. It's still there."

"Was he rich?"

"He had just enough vines to make his own wine. They say he regretted emigrating, but he made money in a San Diego real estate boom, and my father became a doctor, and here I am."

"I'm uncertain."

"Then why do it?"

"It's gone so far. The families have it all settled, especially what *they're* going to wear. Besides, I don't want to hurt Bob."

"Why not stay away another year? He'll wait, won't he?"

"I haven't any talent."

"We all have uncertainties."

"Is studying all you've done?"

"The first year. Since then I have had some interruptions."

"Interesting ones?"

"Educational ones. I'm not the same as when I first arrived in Europe."

"Women?"

"Women."

"I can listen."

"Let's walk. It would be too long a story."

I went with her along Piccadilly as far as Fortnum and Mason's where she was to meet her mother. I believed that this would be our only meeting; and then, as we were saying good-bye, something made me ask, almost against my will,

"Would you like to see the Tate?"

"With you?"

"Who else?"

110

"I thought maybe you were arranging a tour for lonely women."

"Meet me at Amexco again tomorrow at eleven."

"It sounds lovely."

That evening I dithered. I did not want an affair involving my cousin. I went so far as to draft a telegram saying I had been called away. It sounded flimsy. I tore it up. I went to sleep dreaming of Martha's lower lip.

We met on another hot morning, and Martha was again dressed in cool linen with bare legs and sandaled feet, like a flower amidst the wilted tourist throng, her homely face lit and friendly, as we came together in the crowded lobby. My inertia vanished as I realized that I, too, was lonely for someone from home.

We walked to the bottom of the Haymarket and boarded a Number 32 bus, climbed to the top and sat behind the windscreen as the red monster rolled through Trafalgar Square, down Whitehall, past Westminster Abbey, and along Millbank to the riverside Tate Gallery, its Portland stone a dirty gray from London's grime.

The interior was cool and colorful. We wandered through rooms of Turners, the pre-Raphaelites, and contemporary British painters, pausing before Stanley Spencer's fantastic "Resurrection," coming at last to the rooms of the French Impressionists. There Martha's grip on my arm tightened and I felt her response as we walked past the glowing walls of Renoir nudes, Gauguin's tawny Tahitians, the golden checkerboards and blue mountains of Cezanne's Provençal landscapes, Vincent's grain fields and wind-blown cypresses and little yellow chair, the ballet girls and beer drinkers of Dégas, and last of all, a Monet painting of blue poplars against white clouds.

Now Martha was pressed against me, her body like a harp under the touches of form and color. Thus had Erda responded to music. I knew that we were moving toward denouement. We did not speak. Painting was our tongue.

We stopped on the way out to look at the sculpture in the foyer—a stone woman with crushed lips and breasts by

Gaudier-Brjeska called "Chanteuse Triste;" a crucifixion and an Eve by Eric Gill, demonstrating his twin loves for the religious and the erotic; Rodin's "Fallen Caryatid" and his head of Balzac.

When I saw that she liked these last pieces, I suggested that we go next to the Victoria and Albert Museum and see the collection of sculptures given by Rodin during the World War.

"We haven't eaten," I reminded her.

"You have fed me."

And so we walked hand in hand along the Embankment in the shade of the plane trees, seeing the Thames with its traffic of tugs and barges.

I asked directions of a bobby at the Albert Bridge, and then we boarded the bus that took us via the Marble Arch and Kensington to the Victoria and Albert. There we spent an hour in the cool dark rooms of the Museum where sunlight never reached, looking at the Rodins and the replicas of Florentine bronzes by Donatello and Giambologna. Martha paused in front of Rodin's "Fallen Angel," a bronze of two women in an intertwined position, their mouths joined, one woman on her back, bent like a bow.

"I am not sure that I like it," she said.

I ran my hands over the cold metal. "He was a bull of a man. I can see him tearing the two apart and making love to them separately."

"It's a wonder the English would allow it."

"The title puts them off. They think it's something from Milton."

She laughed.

We left the museum and crossed to Hyde Park and lay on the grass in the shade of great poplars. People drifted around us, dogs played, and in the distance the buses honked like geese.

"My feet are hot," Martha said.

"Let me unbuckle your sandals."

I held her bare foot in my hands and massaged it gently, then the other. She lay back and closed her eyes.

"It's lovely," she murmured.

"The feet are generally neglected. Men think hands are the only things worth holding."

"I never knew I could feel close to someone so quickly."

"Art does it."

"I'm glad you're not on the make."

"I thought maybe I was."

"Well, not obviously."

"There are other ways to make love than pushing a woman down on her back."

"How did you know the way to a woman's heart is through her feet?"

"A footnote in Gray's *Anatomy*."

She laughed. "Bob would think we're crazy."

"Art intoxicates."

"Art and Jack. I hate not being a good painter."

"Being a good woman comes first."

"What is good?"

"Said jesting Cameron and would not stay for an answer."

"I like you."

"And I you."

"I'm leaving tomorrow night."

"A good thing, too."

"Don't you want me to stay?"

"What would we do?"

"Man leads, woman follows."

"Your hands remind me of Rossetti's *Silent Noon*. 'Your hands lie open in the long fresh grass, the finger points shine through like rosy blooms.'"

"Why didn't you find me in Munich?"

"Je ne sprache pas Deutsch."

"It was a wasted year."

"You'd better marry Bob soon, if you're going to."

"Mother wonders why I toss and turn at night. I can't talk to her, she's such a prude. She told me once her husband had never seen her naked. I hate what she did to him. He was once a virile man, I know. Now he's her eunuch. She said she wouldn't sleep in the same room with me if I didn't wear a

nightgown."

"You sleep naked?"

"Don't you?"

"In weather like this."

"Bob's a prude, too."

"I don't know him at all. I already know you much better."

"We met only yesterday. It didn't take long, did it?"

"I know that the relationship between a man and a woman, the physical act, can be the most beautiful thing on earth. Not automatically and not always. Rarely, I guess. But then it can be so intense and creative as to make all the forms of art which flow from it mere echoes and reflections."

"You speak with conviction."

"Being in Europe has taught me everything."

"Tell me some you've learned."

"I can't tell it. I can only be it."

"I think I know what you mean."

The hot afternoon passed and we had neither lunch nor tea. We lay on the grass and talked and were silent, talked more and then dozed, in "a close-companioned inarticulate hour, when twofold silence was the song of love."

"Can we have supper together?" I asked, as we finally rose to leave.

"Mother has theater tickets. Dine with us at the hotel. Mother would like to meet you."

"Would I like mother?"

"No." She took my hand. "But you like me; you said you did."

"I do. You lead now and I'll follow."

We walked through Kensington Gardens, past the duck pond, the statue of Peter Pan and the sunken garden, to her hotel.

Mrs. Cameron was a reserved woman. I could strike no sparks from her, and we were able to converse at all only when I steered the talk to the subject of her own health.

Then we were saying good-bye in the lobby and again Martha's widened eyes spoke to me, and I heard myself asking her to dine with me the following evening.

"I'm sorry," Mrs. Cameron replied, "tomorrow is our last day. We are going to Hampton Court and won't be back until late. Our boat train leaves at one a.m. Something about the *Mauretania* sailing with the tide. Martha couldn't possibly see you again, Dr. Burgoyne."

She held out her hand. I ignored it and looked at Martha. She had blanched so that the freckles were jumping off her face. She looked at her mother, then at me. The denouement still lay ahead. I would not be denied.

"What time will you be back?" I asked Martha.

"By six."

"Meet me in front of Selfridge's at seven-thirty. I know a French restaurant you'll love. And there's Duke Ellington at the Palladium. I'll get you to the boat train on time. Your mother can take the bags in a cab. After all, Bob asked *me* to look after you in London."

Mrs. Cameron was speechless.

"I'm going to do it, mother. I'm not going to sit around this hotel until midnight."

Mrs. Cameron turned her back and went to the lift. Martha seized my hand. Her eyes were enormous.

"Thank God! I would have backed down."

"Pour Robert et pour la patrie. Do you want to see me a last time?"

She squeezed my hand. "Guess."

The next day seemed endless. I tried to bury the thought of Martha, the coolness of her garb, her fair freckled skin, widened eyes and bee-stung lip and the feel of her naked feet in my hand, but her image burned in me like a live coal.

Yet I made no plans. How could I? I had little money and less time. I sought to pass the day by walking, clear to St. Paul's, and there with a guide up onto the catwalk around the base of the dome from where we could see for miles around.

I returned to my lodging for tea and cucumber sandwiches, shaved again, took a bath and donned fresh clothes, and was waiting in front of Selfridge's in Oxford Street when Martha stepped off the bus. She was wearing a gray woolen skirt and a short-sleeved purple cashmere pullover, sandals on her bare

feet. Her expectant face was lovely to see.

"Not too tired?" I asked.

"Oh Jack, why did you wait until the very last minute to ask me? Didn't you know I was praying all through dinner for you to ask me out my last night in London?"

"Is your mother still angry?"

"I shouldn't tell you this, but coming back on the boat, do you know what she said? She said she would be happier if I were marrying someone more mature than Bob. Someone like Dr. Burgoyne."

"You made that up."

"You buffaloed her."

"What did you say?"

"I said I didn't know anyone like Dr. Burgoyne."

"You'll be happy with Bob once you're married."

"He cabled that he's meeting the boat in New York."

"Don't give up your painting."

"When do you leave?"

"Next Thursday on the *Loch Clair*. It takes a whole month to San Pedro."

"I wish, I wish . . ."

"Dreamer."

We walked through Oxford Circus and on to Bloomsbury and the French restaurant in Charlotte Street called "Chez Antoine." There we sat at one of four candle-lit tables on the privet-hedged *terrasse*, and after plates of leek and potato soup, we ate cold roast beef, sliced cucumbers and tomatoes and French bread, and drank a bottle of chilled vin rosé. The garçon was pleased by the relish with which we dispatched the food.

"You're a healthy one," I observed, as we finished with coffee and cognac.

"Witty, not pretty."

"More beautiful each time."

"It's you."

"It was a long day."

"You wanted me to come."

"I wanted nothing else."

"You seem so serene about everything."

"I wasn't today. I could hardly wait for you to come down river. Now the time will pass too fast. What shall we do?"

"What *can* we do?"

"The Duke's at the Palladium. Want to go?"

"Do you?"

"I want what you want."

"Then can't we just talk? Maybe walk somewhere?"

"How did you know that's what I really want to do?"

"You make me feel that we're doing what I want to do, and yet I know that it's you who's leading. You know what a woman wants."

"What does a woman want?"

"Strength that's gentle."

"I didn't always know it."

"Live and learn."

"Live and love."

"I'm afraid it's too late."

It was nearly ten o'clock by the time we had finished the coffee and a second cognac. It was still twilight. The moon had risen from behind the row of high dwellings across the narrow street. Antoine came out for a breath of air. When he greeted us in French, I replied in his tongue.

"I thought you were French," he said, "but I cannot determine your region."

"California."

"But that is in America."

"I am American, but my paternal grandfather was French. He lived in Auxerre and made his own wine. Mademoiselle's father lives in California and makes his own wine. She and I drink the wine that others make."

"You have both the form and the spirit of a Frenchman. You are also an artist."

"I am a scientist. Mademoiselle is the artist. She is a painter."

"Many painters live in Charlotte Street. Your Whistler had his studio across from us. What does Mademoiselle paint?"

"He wants to know what you paint," I said to her in English.

"I am old-fashioned enough," she replied, "to believe that the human body is the best subject."

"But of course," Antoine agreed, "providing it is unclothed."

"We need your counsel, patron," I said. "Mademoiselle's boat train departs at one a.m., alas, and before then she wishes to take a walk. For exercise, that is, having eaten this enormous meal. And, I hasten to add, I intend to accompany her, although I ate much more abstemiously."

"Great liar," she said, ruffling my hair.

"She is far too precious and tender a creature," I continued, "to be turned loose in London on a night like this. Can you, will you, patron, in fact, you must recommend a likely promenade."

"No sidewalks or pavements," Martha said. "Remember, I'm a country girl from Calistoga."

"It is true, patron," I said. "This delicate slip of a thing was actually born and raised in a vineyard. For all I know, she was conceived in one."

"How charming," Antoine exclaimed, in English. "How utterly charming. Let me offer a liqueur in the nymph's honor."

"More cognac," Martha growled.

"Three for the road," Antoine roared.

We toasted exuberantly and then Antoine said, "I know the perfect promenade for you two nature-lovers. You are probably aware that London's parks close at nightfall—all but one. Do you know where Primrose Hill is? The other side of Regents Park, not far from the Zoo."

"I love monkeys," Martha said.

"Be serious," Antoine chided, "and hear me out. The Hill is London's only unfenced park. One can walk there all the night long."

"But we haven't all night," I said.

"How far is it?" Martha asked.

"Go to Russell Square and take a 169. It will set you down at the foot of the hill. In this prolonged drought, which I just heard on the news is due momentarily to break; in this dry weather the grass will be likewise."

"I beg your pardon, patron," I said, "It should be em-

phasized that we are friends, not lovers."

Antoine peered at us, then smiled. "It is better to be friends first and lovers afterward, than the other way around."

"You are a philosopher," Martha said.

"I am a Frenchman," Antoine replied, "which is the same thing."

I paid the bill and we set out for Russell Square. The bus came soon and in another twenty minutes we were at the foot of Primrose Hill. We walked arm in arm up the path to the top of the low hill, turned, and saw London far and wide beneath us. The sounds of traffic were muted. The moon was orange colored through the warm air.

"What time is it?" Martha asked.

"Eleven-fifteen."

"Can you keep track? I can't."

"Trust me to."

"I do, oh I do."

"This is our last time."

"I know."

"I'll surely see you again, but it won't be the same, with you Bob's wife."

"I know everything tonight. Remy Martin makes me clairvoyant."

"I'm a wee bit drunk," I confessed.

We walked on over the crest and off the path onto the grass. I reached down and felt it.

"Antoine was right. It's as dry as my mouth."

I took her arm and pulled her gently.

"Sit down here. It won't stain your skirt."

"What's a mere skirt on a night like this?"

She stretched out on her back, arms at her side, and stared at me. I sat down beside her. A faint breeze rustled the may trees. Crickets sang and we heard the sounds of switch engines, shunted cars, and an occasional whistle from a nearby railway yard. The dry grass filled the air with sweetness. I looked down at Martha. She smiled up at me. I lay down beside her. There were no words.

My hand was paralyzed. Only by enormous effort did I

force it to find her bare arm with my fingertips.

"How cool your skin is!"

"Is it as cool as that marble you touched?"

"No, there's fire beneath the skin."

For answer her hand found mine and our fingers joined and began to woo "with the hot blood's blindfold art." I slid my hand beneath her sweater. Her breasts were bare. She began to tremble.

"No," she whispered, rolling free. "It's all or none."

I got up and walked behind a may tree and made water.

When I returned, she had turned on her belly. Again I sat beside her, and now I began to caress the length of her curved body, then gently turned her over and found her lips with mine. Ours was a deep, searching kiss.

She finally broke away. "If you do," she said, "I'll never leave you."

"Good," I said. "I'll never let you go."

I drew her roughly to me and again we kissed with hungry relief. We had gone over the falls. I had no power to stop, no thought of anything but the gift of her body, now open, arched and ready, the flesh on fire, burning, burning.

Then I heard a cough nearby. I started up. There at a respectful distance stood two helmeted bobbies. I waited, thinking they would move along. They did not. I helped Martha to her feet and we adjusted our clothes. The bobbies saluted and went on and took position at a respectful distance.

We walked back down the hill. In the arc light at the foot I dared look at my watch. Twelve-fifteen. We ran along Park Row until we reached the cab rank. A single vehicle was there. I spoke to the venerable driver.

"Waterloo Station. A one o'clock boat train. Can you make it?"

"With minutes to spare, sir," was the confident reply, and away we chugged through the quiet streets.

Martha lay in my arms and we kissed. Her face was wet with tears.

"Because I'm happy," she said when I sought to comfort her. "It was decided for us."

"There was no virtue in me," I said.

"I was yours, all yours."

"You've kept your promise to Bob."

"Hold me, darling, all the way. You don't feel cheated?"

"A thousand times no. It was more wonderful than any loving I've ever known."

"Remember, when you see us go down the aisle."

"Darling, darling, my beautiful darling!"

We reached Waterloo Station at quarter to one. I tipped the driver half a crown and we rushed through the swarming station to the boat-train gate. There Mrs. Cameron fell on us with a cry of relief.

"I told you I would," I said. "Here's your darling daughter and all in one piece."

"God knows what you two have been up to," she said. "Martha's hair is a fright. And is that grass on her skirt?"

"Dry grass," Martha laughed, as we ran along the platform to Mrs. Cameron's compartment.

We boarded with minutes to spare, then Martha walked back to the vestibule with me and we kissed good-bye with hunger and tenderness in our touch.

Back on the platform I stood beneath their compartment. Martha put down the window and reached her hand to me. Her face was transfigured. Her lips kept soundlessly saying my name. The train began to move. I walked along still holding her hand, until we were pulled apart.

I watched the Southampton Express go by, its cream and red cars bearing the Cunard arms on their sides. Swift and swifter and then gone and the coal smoke drifting back. For the first time I felt cold sober.

I walked across Waterloo Bridge to Piccadilly and the all-night Lyons Corner House, and here I took the same table where we had lunched so long ago, only two days ago. I laid my hands palm down on the cold marble, and when the waitress came for my order, I said, "All I want, please, is a bowl of bread and milk."

"I say, that's sensible. You'll sleep well, sir. I always take one at the end of my day."

"It was beginning to rain as I came in."

"Pshaw, we planned a Sunday picnic. Now the grass will be wet."

"You should have gone tonight. The grass was dry."

She looked closely at me. "Are you from the country, sir?"

"Yes, I am. From Primrose Hill."

She laughed and went for my order.

AFTERWORD

in a letter to the author
from

HENRY MILLER

May 29, 1943
The Glen

Dear Larry,

I'm glad I had the chance to reread your book: it seems even better to me on second reading. For me it is the only book by an American which deals with *les amourettes*; it is also the first book by an American which gives to these little, passing loves the proper frame, the proper fragrance. It occupies a realm which is quite blank in our literature; it has a pagan, sophisticated quality which removes it from the sentimental or the immoral. It is thoroughly amoral—and aesthetic; its contour is spherical, finite and melodious. Each episode carries its own carnal glow; in each there is a blossoming, a ripening and a death. It is on the level of nature throughout, and it is this which gives one such a good feeling on putting the book down. It is true also that it is permeated with that melancholy which inspired the phrase—*la chair est triste*.

There are so many things about your book I like and admire that I scarcely know where to begin. Perhaps it has a special charm for me because of its European setting. Everything you refer to in your excursions and explorations, all your little observations, your discoveries and delights, I share intimately. In reading you I relive my own life abroad. With this difference—that I like your life better. I like what I must

123

curiously call the "chaste" aspect. Behind the ardent lover there is always the serious student, and behind him the strange American that all of us are. For we are a strange species when set down in a foreign land. We are so awkward, so stupidly earnest, so childishly hungry, so inept, so inflexible. And yet we are loved, whenever we give the foreigner a chance to know us, to see into our hearts. And we are loved, and eventually respected, precisely for that quality which your Jack Burgoyne is always revealing—*tenderness*. That is the one thing we have to offer to the European woman. And it is something for which she seems to be perpetually craving.

In the episode which concerns Madeleine Montrechet, for me the peak of the book, I was shocked at first, and then suddenly thrilled, to find your hero reading to her from "Lady Chatterley's Lover." It was *her* book, I know, and perhaps that is why I read with such expectancy. What a strange figure this Mellors must have seemed to her! But what Mellors had was tenderness—and humor. No one has emphasized that enough, in studying this curious book of Lawrence's. It was the death-blow to the sickly English sentimentality which pervades their romances. And it is a humor unthinkable to a Mediterranean people, where carnal love is concerned. But, once again, I must compliment you on a little observation—which Madeleine makes when you take her to Villefranche to see the *Rex* lying at anchor in the bay. No love-making outdoors! It's unnatural! How French, that! And how right—for them. In the Lawrence book it was almost necessitous—to take Lady Chatterley outdoors and tumble her over. It was necessary to bring the pale, sickly English body out into the sunshine, to expose it to the light, to weld it to the sun-beaten earth which it had forgotten.

And while on this subject of Lawrence, how grateful I am to you for including the passage from "Apocalypse." How many times I have read that particular passage. Each phrase is burned into my memory. Nowhere in Lawrence is there anything to compare with this for truth and poignancy. It is as though he added something to the Bible, a coda concerning the flesh which had been overlooked by those who thought

only of man's soul. "Man wants his physical fulfillment first and foremost, since now, once and once only, he is in the flesh and potent." What Lawrence forgot, in speaking of man's not wanting his own isolate salvation of his soul, is that in other times, other religions—I am thinking of India particularly— man did find salvation, fulfillment and God through love. The Hindus had their Bhakti Yoga as well as all the other forms of yoga. In Hindu lore the great love unions ended in bliss, in a sort of deification of flesh and spirit. In the West the great love sagas end in agony and death. But that, it seems to me, was always the fault of the man. He could not carry the woman through to the heavenly gates; he foundered in the sexual embrace.

But to return to specific delights . . . . This peculiar charm of the American abroad, which so many writers have treated of—Henry James at one pole and Mark Twain at the other—what a pleasure you give us in observing *l'education sentimentale* of Jack Burgoyne! Very wise of you to round it off with a quintet. Just as in the musical form, there is in these five episodes a true progression. There is a beginning which is harsh and strident and an end which is utterly harmonious in its unresolved fulfillment. The whole development reveals precisely what a book of this sort should reveal—mastery. Mastery in the art of love, I mean. It was absolutely fitting that the penultimate episode should revolve around the very womanly figure of Madeleine Montrechet. It was like an enriching and deepening of the second movement, with Erda. Two earth feelings—one of the cold North, one of the warm Mediterranean. Erda gives the body, but the soul is not yet awake. Madeleine warms the body with spirit. But with Madeleine, as one so often discovers in this region, there is always the thought of "decay," of the fading of powers and the loss of beauty. There is a scepticism born of the sun's fierce heat, a false knowledge of death, I might say. How accurate was your intuition in making those two references to death in this episode. Particularly the latter one, when she comes to you after washing the corpse!

But the greatest delight which the book brings is the at-

mosphere that permeates it. A gentle, soothing atmosphere, even though it be the bleak winter of Dijon or the mean, rainy season of Paris. An atmosphere in which food and wines play an important role. Your cafés are especially redolent. Even the station buffets. And how wonderful it is to go with you to the station and watch the express or the "rapide" shoot by! In every chapter there are trains, it seems: always "le voyage," always "le depart." These night trains come and go, flash like meteors across the sky. Thank you for making the trains come alive! Beautiful objects they are; each time we take one they carry with them some precious part of us.

Yes, there are two atmospheres always—the one through which the story is moving and the other which accompanies it like a refrain, the one evoked by longing and desire, or by pain and remembrance. "The Morvan country lay to the west . . . ." You have no idea how enchanting it is to come upon such an observation. A few lines and we are webbed in Celtic magic and imagery. Or take your frequent little references to the names of those who once lived here—of Rameau making his music in Dijon, of Henry James penning the last lines of his book on a certain bench, of the two famous lovers who spent a night in an old house. Or the "flowery Chablis" which made the nostrils of the other diners expand with pleasure. Or the reference to Vézelay and her Romanesque basilica. Or the blonde Vézelise beer of Dijon. Or you go into the hills near Grasse and you remember to gather a large sachet of wild lavender which is then in bloom. Or you stand on the beach near Cagnes and sling pebbles. Or you return and find her standing against the mimosa, her face uplifted to the moon. And you say—"The still air was heavy with the mingled scent of mimosa, eucalyptus, rose-geranium and sea wrack." Sea wrack! How lucky to recall that! How disturbing and just! Or to think to remind us of "the limestone walls of the Ouche." Everything brings us back to the senses and to their importance not only in art but love. So that when we come to the Rodin figure it is indispensable that you caress it with your hands, as later you will caress the flanks of the one you are making love to. Always a "making love"—a making love "to"

126

and "with." Is it not one of the first things we Americans learn on reaching France—the meaning of *faire l'amour?* A making and a doing—something plastically creative—not just a state of being, however intoxicating. How grateful we were to discover that every French lover is if not an artisan an artist, or vice versa. It is as though we discovered that in love we had existed without arms or legs, that in conversation we had never enjoyed the experience of using the hands, the fingers, to say nothing of the face muscles.

Yes, food and wine, excursions to *la campagne*—and books and music. In every situation there is an ambiance in which the total being participates. It is this perpetual ambiance—like a perpetual temperature—which makes these episodes anything but obscene in character. All of them pivot on sex, true. In all of them it is the taking of the citadel which is paramount, yet how unimportant that becomes if we but glance from the bed and take register of the opaque atmosphere in which all is swimming. How beautiful those little moments by the big window—all Dijon outside, a museum of statues and light, a city groaning with fine wines and with memories of a splendid past. You stand by the window inhaling the fragrance of the street and it is so infinitely more than anything the girl can ever possibly give, though she gave her soul. And how marvelous a mood you evoke when you say of one of your characters—the dipsomaniac—"Each night we did exactly the same things. Beer and talk at the Concorde, steak and red burgundy at the Pré-aux-Clercs, a bottle of mousseux in her room, love-making and sleep." Exactly the regimen for that sort of affair. It will go on and on; it will make no sense to others. And then one day it comes to an abrupt stop. The very repetitiousness is what is exciting. It is like striking the same chord again and again—and then presto! the mood is gone, there is an end—but the memory is hammered in, and when the memory of it returns it is the blood that beats, the blood that remembers.

Perhaps the clue to the beauty of this little book lies in your own words to Martha: "I do know that the physical relationship between a man and a woman can be the most

127

beautiful thing on earth. Simple and beautiful—sometimes. Not every time—just some times." To understand it fully we turn in our minds to some anterior epoch, to one of those periods when the adoration of woman, flowering from the myth of the Virgin, was coupled with a marriage between the male and the female minds. There was a period, we like to think, when Love was enthroned. A period when marriages were consummated first in Paradise, soul meeting soul, and then again the flesh. But the road to the fleshly union lay through the mind. A mind trying earnestly to recapture the flavor of the past. You express it quite beautifully yourself. "Perhaps we are like Paolo and Francesca. Dante tells how they were reading together in the garden one day, and when they came to a certain passage they turned and kissed. Then they laid aside the book and read no more that day." A little *aperçu* such as this speaks volumes. It is as if now, in our own time, walled up in some ugly prison, we catch through the bars of our oubliette a fleeting glimpse of love enacted with passion and faith and intelligence. Then love was a global trine and the consummation was complete in every realm—or failed utterly, so that even the earth was mired. A man or a woman's portrait was made against a magical landscape; the human being was an integral part of that landscape.

Well, Larry, I suppose I could go on indefinitely. Enough, however, to show you how much I appreciate what you have attempted. It is the sort of book I should like to present to those about to venture into the realm of love. A little handbook, a manual of love, to replace the ancient Kama Sutra which was meant to be instructive and not pornographic.

Henry

Printed February 1977 in Santa Barbara and Crawfordsville
for Capra Press by Mackintosh & Young and R. R. Donnelley
& Sons. Design by Dick Palmer. Two hundred copies, spe-
cially bound, have been signed and numbered by the author.